Explosion in
Halifax Harbour
~ 1917 ~

Dan Soucoup

NIMBUS
PUBLISHING LTD

Nimbus Publishing Limited
3731 Mackintosh St, Halifax, NS B3K 5A5
(902) 455-4286 nimbus.ca

Printed and bound in Canada

NB1342

Cover design: Heather Bryan
Interior design: Grace Laemmler

Library and Archives Canada Cataloguing in Publication

Soucoup, Dan, 1949-, author
Explosion in Halifax Harbour, 1917 / Dan Soucoup.

(Stories of our past) Includes bibliographical references and index.
ISBN 978-1-77108-554-0 (softcover)

1. Halifax Explosion, Halifax, N.S., 1917. I. Title. II. Series: Stories of our past (Halifax, N.S.)

FC2346.4.S685 2017   971.6'22503   C2017-904104-5

Nimbus Publishing acknowledges the financial support for its publishing activities from the Government of Canada through the Canada Book Fund (CBF) and the Canada Council for the Arts, and from the Province of Nova Scotia. We are pleased to work in partnership with the Province of Nova Scotia to develop and promote our creative industries for the benefit of all Nova Scotians.

MIX
Paper from
responsible sources
FSC
www.fsc.org   FSC® C103113

CONTENTS

"All this happened in the twinkling of an eye; and in its suddenness and extent the disaster surpassed anything experienced in France or Belgium."

—Prime Minister and Halifax Member of Parliament Robert Borden.

CHAPTER 1

THE HARBOUR

Convoy in Bedford Basin during the Second World War, 1942. This photo, looking towards the Narrows, Halifax peninsula, and the Atlantic Ocean, shows the fabulous size of the inner basin of Halifax Harbour.

THE HALIFAX HARBOUR, THE LARGEST and deepest natural harbour on the Atlantic coast, faces the open ocean and extends a total of thirty-two kilometres from Chebucto Head to the mouth of the Sackville River. Farther inland sits the Bedford Basin—once a pre-glacial river, then an ancient freshwater lake, then, more preciously, a series of lakes after the ice age receded. As the ocean rose about five thousand years ago, the Narrows of the harbour flooded to create the saltwater basin of today. Three kinds of bedrock, called the Halifax Formation, characterize the harbour's geological structure: slate, quartzite, and granite. Fertile drumlins moulded into hills by glaciers are present on both Georges Island and McNabs Island, as well as at Fort Needham on the Halifax peninsula. Today, the Sackville River flows into Bedford Basin where a deep channel drains through the basin and the Narrows close to the Dartmouth shore, before turning west of Georges and McNabs islands, flowing out by Herring Cove and Chebucto Head and into the Atlantic Ocean.

This grand harbour—known as Chebooktook or Chebucto, meaning "big" to the first inhabitants of the region—remains ice-free most winters. The nearby warm waters of the Gulf Stream heat the south-flowing Arctic currents to modify the Nova Scotia climate. Halifax's harbour is also unique in that it narrows well inside the inner harbour and opens again, hourglass-like, into a huge basin surrounded by hills. This sheltered basin was large enough to hide entire fleets from enemy coastline patrols, which made Chebucto a great naval asset in the age of European expansion.

EARLY PEOPLE

In ancient times, about 5000 BC, early ancestors of the Mi'kmaq began to summer at Halifax Harbour to hunt sea mammals and harvest seafood. Winters were spent inland and two historic waterways transported these first peoples back and forth. Old campsites at the mouth of the Sackville River point to an Indigenous portage route to the Annapolis Valley. And on the Dartmouth shore, at Tufts Cove and Dartmouth Cove, two small rivers lead back to

Mi'kmaq encampment at Tufts Cove, looking towards Halifax c.1837. This oil on canvas painting is attributed to William Eager.

the Shubenacadie lakes, where one could reach the Bay of Fundy in two days of good paddling.

In the 1800s, Indigenous communities existed on both sides of the harbour—including at Armdale in Halifax and Red Bridge Pond and Miller's Mountain in Dartmouth—but by the early 1900s most had vanished. A flourishing settlement comprising sixteen Mi'kmaw families under the leadership of Jerry Lonecloud remained at Turtle Grove near Tufts Cove on the Dartmouth shore.

The Mi'kmaq lived in birchbark wigwams in summer and wooden houses in the colder months, earning money making baskets, paddles, and oars. And their handcrafted hockey sticks were also well regarded throughout Nova Scotia—even nearby Starr Manufacturing was producing a popular Mic-Mac brand stick.

While the 4.5-hectare site at Turtle Grove offered little agricultural potential, it did have a small school donated by Mi'kmaw landowner William Nevins. But white encroachment continued to negatively affect the community, perhaps because the land had easy access to the harbour. By 1917, the federal government had been working with Chief Lonecloud and the band to relocate to two possible sites: one nearby at Albro Lake and another at Shubenacadie.

CHAPTER 2

FOUNDED IN CONFLICT

Town and harbour of Halifax from Georges Island looking north with Dartmouth shore on right, 1759. The British fleet is bound for the siege at Quebec during the Seven Years' War. Drawing by Richard Short, purser aboard HMS *Prince of Wales*.

HALIFAX WAS ESTABLISHED IN 1749 as a British military port to counter the French presence at Louisbourg and Quebec. English-speaking settlements south of Acadie were thriving, but France was contesting British military authority in North

America and Acadie had become the latest battleground. Under Colonel Edward Cornwallis, an expedition of fifteen vessels and approximately 2,500 settlers left England, arriving at Chebucto Harbour on June 21, 1749. Upon landing they proceeded to erect a garrisoned settlement of about eight hectares on a side hill next to the water. Cornwallis's men fortified the hilltop overlooking the town by building log forts and palisades, the site of which would become known as Citadel Hill. The new town was named in honour of Lord Halifax, president of the Board of Trade and Plantations.

Many of these first settlers were inexperienced Londoners who were less than excited about enduring the harsh conditions of the new colony. Some escaped to more prosperous towns in the American colonies, but more settlers—European Protestants and hardy New Englanders—arrived, establishing themselves north of Halifax as well as across the harbour at Dartmouth. These so-called "foreign" Protestants contributed greatly to the fortifications and public infrastructure of early Halifax.

Within a decade, Halifax was at war—there were dozens of British ships-of-the-line docked in the harbour, and convoys sailed off to attack French positions at Louisbourg and Quebec.

The naval dockyard as well as the military garrison was quickly established and expanded as Halifax played host to numerous British war parties. The British routed the French and then attempted, unsuccessfully, to enforce their authority in the rebellious thirteen colonies to the south. The town's raison d'être was to serve the strategic interests of Britain. Over the decades, Halifax's fortunes would soar or decline depending on royal military campaigns. As one writer noted, "For more than 150 years the Imperial Army and Navy had been the lifeblood of the town." Yet in peacetime, the town would almost sleep, springing to life once conflict arose. When squadrons appeared in the harbour, business followed. More than once, as the North Atlantic's staging ground for British military campaigns, Halifax would earn its reputation as the warden of the north.

But as the town expanded north of its original protected borders, the Indigenous populations were less than welcoming, as a foreign power was now claiming their summer fishing grounds. Outraged, the Mi'kmaq protested the very establishment of Halifax, sending a letter to Cornwallis declaring the town's land to be unceded territory. Governor Cornwallis was a military man first, determined to impose his might on anyone—Indigenous or French—not willing to submit to the British crown. After brutal skirmishes during which Cornwallis offered a reward for Mi'kmaw scalps, the Mi'kmaq's French allies were defeated and neutral Acadians exiled, leaving many Mi'kmaq with no choice but to flee for more remote regions of Nova Scotia.

North end Halifax looking south to Citadel Hill from Fort Needham, c.1780. The naval yard is visible on the Halifax shore while Georges Island appears in the background. Illustration by Edward Hicks.

CHAPTER 3

GROWTH AND EXPANSION

AFTER THE WAR OF 1812, a long period of peace ensued and Britain's commitment to Halifax's fortifications waned. During those years, Halifax was incorporated into a city, and by 1841 was progressing on other fronts as well. Nova Scotia's fight for responsible government was noteworthy, the first colony in Canada to have an executive governing council formed from the elected majority party. As well, Halifax became the first North American port to receive mail service from Samuel Cunard's revolutionary steamer *Britannia*.

With the American Civil War raging south of the border, threats were made to invade British North America. But Britain's answer was to orchestrate the merger of its colonies into a dominion, rather than once again build up the town's defenses.

Prior to Confederation, the Nova Scotia Railway was established with the Halifax terminal in the north end of the city, at the bottom of Duffus Street. Known as the Richmond Depot—a much larger one was built at the foot of North Street in 1877—the railway did much to develop the city's north end.

With a railway to Central Canada and the National Policy—a Canada-first plan that placed high tariffs on foreign-manufactured items but not on raw materials—in place, export-oriented industries were established, along with modest homes to house the workers. The typical north-end resident was blue collar, with Irish or Scottish roots, and worked as a labourer

The grand station at the foot of North Street was opened by Prime Minister Alexander Mackenzie in 1877 and featured a 122-metre passenger structure with twenty-four iron trusses supporting a glass-covered roof. The roof would collapse in the explosion killing sixty workers while the five-storey King Edward also suffered damages. What remained of the railway station was demolished and a new terminal was erected in the south end.

or tradesman at one of the many factories in the area.

Another development that played a central role in the north end's growth was the dry dock, erected in 1889 at the foot of Young Street. The Graving Dock could repair the new ironclads and helped spur heavy industry to locate to the north end. Also on the waterfront, close to Pier 8, was the eight-storey Acadia Sugar Refinery (the attached filter house was ten-storeys), then the tallest structure in the Maritimes. Other major industrial progressions included the Hillis & Sons Foundry and the Richmond Printing Company. After a railway spur line was built from the Bedford Basin and along Kempt Road to Robie Street, the Nova Scotia Cotton Manufacturing Company was erected at the corner of Robie and Young Streets employing three hundred people. Also nearby, the Nova Scotia Paint Works was a large operation as well as the Nova Scotia Car Works, which produced between three thousand and four thousand freight cars a year.

By the Edwardian Age (1901–1910), Halifax's north end had transformed from a semi-rural patch of scraggy fields and little farms to a sprawling industrial suburb, extending about five kilometres from Citadel Hill to the Bedford Basin. Richmond was considered the area from North Street to Africville. Along the harbour, a patchwork of streets and roads with various names had sprung up. It was indeed confusing and in 1917, the entire thoroughfare from Point Pleasant Park to Fairview was changed to Barrington Street.

HMS *Ariadne*, coaling at the Halifax dockyard looking north to the Acadia Sugar Refinery, c.1898. Tufts Cove on the Dartmouth shore can be just seen between ships.

AFRICVILLE

While Nova Scotia's treatment of the Mi'kmaq was less than admirable, black Nova Scotians also suffered severe neglect and mistreatment. Slavery "officially" ended in the colony in 1808, but the marginal land African Nova Scotians received after coming to Nova Scotia as free citizens proved inadequate for farming. In frustration, many of these early Black Loyalists left Nova Scotia for Sierra Leone in 1792. Another group, the Black Maroons from Jamaica, also left in 1800. As well, a group of black American refugees arrived during the War of 1812. Many settled in Preston and Hammonds Plains, but also in other Nova Scotia towns such as Amherst, Truro, New Glasgow, and Kentville. For many decades these settlers were unable to acquire legal title to their rural properties, due to the colour of their skin. Many gave up and settled in Halifax and Dartmouth attempting to earn a living.

Most of the refugees lived in north-end Halifax around Creighton and Maynard Streets, but by the 1840s, about eighty were living on the shores of Bedford Basin. Originally part of Campbell Town on Campbell Road—leading to Barrington Street and downtown Halifax—the community gradually became known as Africville. It was split in two in 1854 when the railway cut through the village to the Richmond terminal. Other affronts to the community included dumping the city's trash nearby, establishing Rockhead Prison and the Infectious Diseases Hospital in the neighbourhood, as well as a slaughterhouse, oil and coal storage facilities, and a fertilizer plant.

Still Africville grew and developed into a vibrant, four-hundred-strong community with a church, school, and other amenities including electricity and phone lines. Yet sewer and water were never installed, despite adjacent white communities receiving the services. In the 1960s, city council voted to demolish Africville in favour of relocating the people to other sites in metro Halifax. It was the era of urban renewal in North America plus one major

Africville on the shores of Bedford Basin, 1965. This bird's-eye-view photo by Bob Brooks is looking over north end Halifax, with the Narrows and Dartmouth in the background. Part of the Macdonald Bridge is on the right while the MacKay Bridge over the Narrows is still a decade away.

planning reported identified the land as having strong industrial potential. By 1967, the community had been destroyed while the government forced residents into public housing.

DARTMOUTH

In 1873 Dartmouth became incorporated as a town with local industrialist W. S. Symonds as warden. Without access to rail, the town's industries set up near the waterfront. These included

View from a Dartmouth park looking out to the harbour. The ferry is on the right with Georges Island in the background.

shipbuilders, the Symonds Iron Foundry, Dominion Molasses, and John P. Mott's chocolate, soap, and candle factory. By 1900, after two railway bridges had collapsed in the harbour, a railway spur line was built from Windsor Junction. This allowed a number of large industries, like the Acadia Sugar Refinery, Starr Manufacturing, Consumers Cordage (Stairs Ropeworks), and the Oland Brewery, to operate successfully outside the downtown core.

Powered by a dam on Albro Lake, Consumers Cordage on Wyse Road was Dartmouth's largest employer with several hundred workers. It was the longest building in Nova Scotia where rope was mechanically twisted. And on the waterfront at Turtle Grove, Oland's Army and Navy Brewery had been producing beer since the 1860s.

Dartmouth comprised 5,058 residents according to a 1911 census and was growing as houses and roads began to follow the industries. Another important industry employing almost 1,500 workers was started in 1916 next to the sugar refinery. The petroleum age had begun and with the war, demand for oil products was rapidly escalating. Imperial Oil began constructing a refinery and had erected a workers' community called Imperoyal Village. Surrounded by beautiful lakes, the town became well known as a sporting community with paddling events at the Banook Canoe Club and golf at the popular Brightwood Country Club. With such growth and prosperity, Dartmouth's future as an industrial centre looked promising.

As well, a vibrant ferry service had been established to connect Dartmouth to downtown Halifax. Daily commuters—office workers, high school students, and labourers—travelled across the harbour each day.

December 6, 1917, dawned bright and brisk. Dartmouthians assembled as usual in the new terminal and boarded the next ferry to Halifax a little before nine o'clock. In the cool December morning, they would decide whether to stay inside the ferry cabin or go to the open upper deck and take in the salt air. Once out in the harbour, they could see a burning ship to the north, but knew nothing of the danger lurking.

Vessels identified are HMS *Pallas, Crescent, Diadem, Tribune, Psyche, Proserpine,* and *Indefatigable.* This formidable navy, still the most powerful in the world, would shortly exit its key North American port after more than 150 years.

CHAPTER 4
WAR IN A NEW CENTURY

DURING THE CLOSING DECADES OF the nineteenth century, Britain still maintained a military garrison in Halifax as well as a significant naval presence. Yet Halifax's role as a strategic naval centre had diminished in importance as Britain's new global adversary was now situated close to home. German nationalism was challenging Britain's superiority in Europe, and most military observers predicted the next major conflict would occur far away from the North America theatre. Consequently in 1906, the last British troops left Halifax and the entire fortress, including the Royal dockyard, was turned over to the Dominion of Canada.

So Halifax's old benefactor had quit the city but a new patron from far inland had stepped in and began upgrading the port's infrastructure. In 1910, the federal government in Ottawa announced plans for a modest Canadian navy and the old Royal Navy cruiser *Niobe* was acquired and stationed in Halifax as Canada's first naval vessel in Atlantic waters. A naval college was also established and the port's decrepit facilities were modernized. Concrete piers, deepwater terminals, and new railway lines to service the steamships and ocean liners began to be built. The new docks were deep in the city's south end, and eight kilometres of slate rock were blasted from Fairview to Greenbank at Point Pleasant Park, while sixteen concrete bridges were erected to accommodate the new rail line running behind the city.

The Canadian Garrison Artillery, Detachment #4, 1st Regiment, training at Fort Charlotte, Georges Island in Halifax Harbour, 1914. Mobilized at the beginning of the war, the volunteer regiment saw almost seven hundred men serve overseas and also assisted in relief efforts during the explosion.

THE FIRST WORLD WAR

When the conflict broke out in Europe on July 28, 1914, many could say they were not surprised. And while Canada went to war, it was not prepared for the epic struggle. Britain expected its colonies to contribute supplies and soldiers to the struggle. Old HMCS *Niobe* was now permanently berthed at the Halifax dockyard as a training ship, so the Royal Navy returned to the port. With a fledgling navy, Canada also attempted to contribute to the Allied naval effort and soon had an odd assortment of appropriated fishing vessels and old yachts that became known as the Tin Pot Navy. By late 1917, the RCN had assembled a motley fleet, which included old minesweepers, trawlers, tugboats with mounted cannons, patrol vessels, and even a couple of outdated submarines.

As in past wars, Halifax suddenly sprang to life with large increases in jobs, population, prices, rents, factory orders, and ship repairs. With the new prosperity, the port became one of the busiest anywhere with cargo exports reaching 17 million tons, up from barely 2 million in 1913. Troopships—280,000 military personnel exited the port during the war—convoys, and merchant marine vessels all jammed the harbour while transportation and other city services were unable to keep up with demand from the increased populace.

As Canada's major garrison town, about five thousand soldiers, including Canadian and British regulars plus militia, were housed in Halifax by 1917. Prostitution and liquor sales soared—especially in 1916 when civil authorities mysteriously began enforcing the old temperance act, closing all legitimate drinking establishments in the city. Once the official "dry" policy was enforced, tension between military personal and civil authorities escalated, adding greatly to the stress on city streets. Unaccustomed to such chaos, Haligonians struggled to cope; yet some made a lot of money supplying the military with everything from food to booze by the ton.

WARSHIPS IN HALIFAX HARBOR. HALIFAX, N. S.

The lone Canadian naval vessel on the east coast, *Niobe* was an old Diadem class cruiser that had served the Royal Navy in the Boer War. Obsolete by the First World War, *Niobe* was permanently moored at Pier 4 serving as naval headquarters and training centre for new sailors.

CHAPTER 5

WHO'S IN CHARGE?

AT THE OUTSET OF THE First World War, the federal government had complete control over marine affairs in Halifax Harbour. But the young Royal Canadian Navy was filled with inexperience and these "prairie sailors," while quite keen, were unskilled in saltwater navigation. Local civilian authorities were also involved in shipping matters, but war concerns trumped non-military affairs, and these officials grudgingly lost much of their influence. And having returned to the harbour, the Royal Navy with its curses—blind pigs, bawdy houses, petty crime—but also attributes—unmatched naval superiority, prosperity, and pompous galas—was given full control over convoys and vetting neutral vessels.

But many Royal Canadian Navy officers were retirees from the Royal Navy and deference to the mighty Royal Navy in harbour matters was simply a matter of fact. The RCN's Admiral Charles Kingsmill ran Halifax Harbour from far away Ottawa and became alarmed when Rear Admiral Bertram Chambers, head of the Royal Navy's Halifax operations, was described by the British admiralty as Halifax's senior naval officer afloat. In fact, the rear admiral was most senior but to be considered in charge of everything "afloat" by the world's most powerful navy, certainly undermined Canadian Naval authority, creating what Kingsmill described as "unutterable confusion."

It certainly became complicated since the war had disturbed the command structure, and without the moral authority to act, Canada's Navy still remained officially responsible for

Canadian waters. It was even more baffling when the Americans entered the war in 1917 and began arriving in Halifax only to learn that Canadian authorities controlled harbour issues. As well, the Halifax pilots, responsible for guiding all ocean-going vessels in and out of the harbour, were accustomed to operating with almost full autonomy. Despite the Canadian Navy now being in charge, the fourteen working harbour pilots continued to operate independently. By the fall of 1917, retired British naval officer Frederick Wyatt was the Royal Canadian Navy's chief examining officer (CXO), the de facto harbour master—since the civilian harbour master, Captain Francis Rudolf, was relegated to overseeing local craft.

With offices aboard *Niobe* in Halifax, Wyatt reported to Acting Superintendent Captain Frederick Pasco, considered the Canadian senior naval officer in Halifax. But Wyatt was barely being informed of what ships were coming and going in the harbour. Since 1914, munitions ships were regularly being allowed to enter the harbour without a great deal of precaution and by 1917, were routinely assigned to convoys crossing the Atlantic. This meant dangerous goods being transported in and out of one of the busiest harbours on the Atlantic seaboard.

With so many organizations operating in a semi-autonomous fashion, no one seemed to be fully in charge, and wartime Halifax become a dangerous place.

CHAPTER 6

THE DAY BEFORE THE COLLISION

The Sherbrooke Tower shown here was erected at Maugers Beach in 1828 and was later modified into a lighthouse. In 1851, Abraham Gesner experimented at the site with his new kerosene fuel in attempts to replace whale oil. Lighthouse keeper David George declared kerosene the superior fuel and eventually kerosene powered most lighthouses.

LATE ON DECEMBER 1, 1917, the *Mont Blanc* steamed out of New York and headed north. The 3,121-ton French vessel carried a forty-man crew along with one of the most volatile combinations of high explosives ever packed into a cargo ship.

The munitions freighter, built in England in 1899 and purchased by the French shipping firm Compagnie Générale Transatlantique, carried 2,300 tons of wet and dry picric acid, 200 tons of TNT, 10 tons of gun cotton, and 35 tons of benzol.

Upon arriving in New York, Captain Aimé Le Médec had been informed that he would be transporting a large shipment of explosives to war-torn France, and the cargo was highly dangerous. Before loading, shipwrights constructed special wooden linings in the four holds as well as partitions between decks so the hazardous materials would remain secure and separated at sea. At the time, picric acid was the most sought-after explosive material and benzol was the superior gasoline. Together with the always-dangerous cargo of TNT, Captain Le Médec sailed forth knowing full well the *Mont Blanc* was a powder keg ready to ignite with one false move. Arriving in Halifax Harbour four days later, he handed his papers and cargo manifest to examining officer Terrence Freeman and announced in broken English, "We are all explosives!"

British convoy authorities in New York had been unwilling to allow Captain Le Médec to sail directly in convoy to Europe in his slow munitions ship, and instead sent the *Mont Blanc* to Halifax with instructions to try and find a convoy willing to accommodate the dangerous vessel. *Mont Blanc* was barely capable of averaging seven to ten knots in ideal conditions and would no doubt be left behind in most convoys.

Late in the afternoon of December 5, veteran pilot Francis Mackey boarded the *Mont Blanc* at the mouth of Halifax Harbour. Since the outbreak of the war, Halifax pilots had been working extra hours to try and keep up with the huge increase in shipping. Using pilots to guide ocean-going vessels had been declared compulsory, and Mackey had boarded the *Mont Blanc* directly from an outgoing ship.

With twenty-four years of experience, Francis Mackey had a strong, accident-free résumé. Despite speaking little French while Captain Le Médec only had some fluency in English, the two men certainly understood each other. Le Médec made clear to Mackey what cargo was on board the *Mont Blanc*. Examining service officer Terrence Freeman also learned of Le Médec's freight but because of the late hour, gave instruction to the vessel to anchor just outside the harbour's defence line.

Halifax had two anti-submarine cables that prevented ships from sailing in or out of the harbour after dark. Freeman promised Le Médec that in the morning, his vessel would be allowed to proceed to the convoy-marshalling site in Bedford Basin. Lieutenant Freeman also confirmed the arrival of the *Mont Blanc* and relayed the information of its cargo to Chief Examining Officer Frederick Wyatt. Le Médec and Mackey then settled into the captain's cabin anchored at the Examination Anchorage, within sight of McNabs Island lighthouse.

On the other side of the defence line, the harbour was busy with many ships. The Grace Line freighters *Curaca* (at Pier 8) and *Calonne* (at Pier 9) were both loading horses and prairie wheat destined for Europe. The transatlantic liner RMS *Olympic* was anchored in the Bedford Basin with five thousand Chinese labourers on board. The American hospital ship *Old Colony* was in port and in dry dock receiving repairs, as were the *Hovland* out of Norway, the cargo ship *Middleham Castle*, and the British *Picton*.

HMS *Highflyer*, a 5,600-ton cruiser, lay anchored mid-channel. The warship was slated to escort the next convoy across the Atlantic and was well regarded in Halifax, having sunk the big German ship *Kaiser von der Grosse*. Numerous other vessels plied back and forth around the harbour such as the former minesweeping tug *Stella Maris* and the three hard-working Dartmouth ferries. But there was one vessel anchored in the neutral area near the southwest shore of Bedford Basin that was especially anxious to exit Halifax.

The *Imo* was owned by the Norwegian Southern Pacific Whaling Company but was chartered by the Belgian Relief Commission to transport badly needed supplies from North America across the

Atlantic (via Halifax and New York) to Belgium. With a crew of thirty-nine men and registering 5,041 gross tons, the *Imo*, as a neutral ship, carried no war materials and had *BELGIAN RELIEF* painted on both sides of the vessel in large, capital letters. *Imo* could enter Halifax Harbour for fuel or repairs but as a neutral, its crew was not permitted on land or allowed to speak directly with shore personnel to ensure spying did not take place.

Norwegian Captain Haakon From had been at anchor in the Bedford Basin since December 3 and was impatiently waiting to take on coal before sailing on to New York to pick up more provisions. From had a confined crew and was insisting on departing Halifax on December 5, since customs officer Arthur Lovett had already granted his exit clearance. But the coaling vessel had been late and the *Imo*'s frustrated captain was informed that the submarine net would have to be down before he could set sail. That wouldn't happen until the next morning.

Even though the *Imo* had been cleared to leave Halifax on the fifth, customs officer Lovett had failed to inform harbour authorities that the vessel had, in fact, been delayed. Pilot William Hayes left the vessel for the evening, promising Captain From he would be back at daylight to guide the *Imo* out to sea. He did inform the pilotage office on Bedford Row of the delay.

Whether the pilotage office informed the CXO of the delay is unclear since Frederick Wyatt had only requested to be informed when any ship left the harbour. And this unfortunate postponement, along with the *Mont Blanc*'s delay entering the port, perhaps more than any other factor, led to tragedy. The next morning William Hayes arrived on a Pickford & Black tug as agreed, and the *Imo* was among the early ships to steam out of the basin.

THE COLLISION

Smoke cloud from the explosion floats over the harbour, December 6, 1917. The photo was attributed to a Captain Baird off McNabs Island.

EARLY ON THE COLD, CLEAR morning of December 6, the submarine nets had opened and Captain Le Médec, second in line to enter the harbour behind the American freighter SS *Clara*, received his signal from the gunboat: "Proceed to Bedford and await further orders." Pilot Mackey, aboard the *Mont Blanc* with the captain, instructed Le Médec to steam toward the

Narrows but only at four knots—one knot under the harbour speed limit. Mackey steered the *Mont Blanc* along the Dartmouth side, which would allow outgoing ships to pass on the Halifax side. A crewmember asked if the red flag, signifying explosives on board, should be hoisted. Le Médec declined, knowing that wartime secrecy called for the flag to be flown only when loading hazardous materials.

A little after 8:00 a.m., Captain From, still irritated from missing his exit the previous day, got underway in the Bedford Basin, heading out towards the Narrows. Travelling about seven knots, two above the harbour limit, From was clearly in a hurry. Pilot William Hayes knew his job that morning was to get the *Imo* out of Halifax as quickly as possible. While permission from the guard ship in the basin had cleared the *Imo* for takeoff, the guard ship had no apparent information about incoming traffic, nor had there been any morning communication with CXO Wyatt aboard the *Niobe*.

At the north entrance to the tight channel in the Narrows, vessels heading down-channel toward the ocean must swing left and turn sharply to the Halifax side. But *Imo* was confronted by the incoming SS *Clara*, which was approaching from the port side instead of the starboard. *Clara* pilot Edward Renner signalled that he intended to stay on the Halifax side, producing a quandary for the *Imo*. Pilot Hayes had two options: he could stop the *Imo*'s engines and let the *Clara* pass into the basin—thereby losing more time—or proceed with passing on what was considered, navigationally, the wrong side. Hayes chose the latter action, and *Imo* and *Clara* ended up passing starboard to starboard.

Perhaps Hayes intended to quickly swing back toward the correct side once he passed the *Clara*, but the *Imo* then encountered the tug *Stella Maris* towing two loaded scows from the dockyard into the basin. Commanded by Captain Horatio Brannen, the tug moved closer to the Halifax shore to avoid the *Imo* and in doing so, forced the relief vessel to again move to the Dartmouth side while entering the Narrows.

This heavy traffic could have been the reason *Imo* stayed on the Dartmouth side attempting to exit the harbour. Whatever the reason, the rules of the road were not followed. Later, Captain Brannen recalled his impression that the *Imo* was moving quite quickly. He claimed to have turned to his second mate and said, "She is going as fast as any ship I ever saw in the harbour." Aboard the tugboat *Nereid*, Captain John L. Makiny would later confirm that the *Imo* "had quite a foam on her bow" while in the Narrows.

Meanwhile, the *Mont Blanc* had stopped its engines to allow a passenger ferry to cross from Halifax to Dartmouth. The vessel continued on until Pilot Mackey saw HMS *Highflyer* anchored to port side. The two vessels exchanged flag salutes. Next, Mackey spotted the *Imo* approaching from the Narrows about a kilometre away, but from the Dartmouth side. "Why is he coming down in our waters?" Mackey asked Captain Le Médec. *Mont Blanc* let out one short whistle blast, indicating they had the right of way to pass on the Dartmouth side. To be extra cautious, Mackey decided to take the vessel further toward the Dartmouth shore and reduce speed. Yet to Mackey's dismay, the larger vessel responded with two short blasts, indicating that the *Imo*, too, intended to bear toward Dartmouth.

Charles Duggan, a twenty-year-old north-end ferry operator, had watched harbour traffic for many years from his house window on Richmond's Hanover Street. He noticed with interest that the Belgian relief vessel *Imo* was speeding south outside its lane. *Imo* was close to the Dartmouth side and rather than moving back to the Halifax side, was holding its course. He could see a second freighter approaching *Imo* in the same lane and what worried him most was the Belgian vessel's speed. It was moving at a good clip.

Exasperated, Mackey told the *Mont Blanc*'s captain to again honk one blast, but both Le Médec and Mackey became fearful as the *Imo*, now bearing down on the munitions ship, repeated the two-blast signal indicating it intended to stay the course. Unable to move any further to starboard without grounding, and with the *Imo* closing in on his ship, Pilot Mackey saw his only option to avoid a collision was for the *Mont Blanc* to go to port and allow the *Imo* to pass between his ship and the Dartmouth shore.

Mackey himself rang the whistle twice to signal his intention to move over while Captain Le Médec gave the order to "bear to the left." *Mont Blanc* was almost at a standstill, yet the laden vessel still managed to turn toward the Halifax shore bringing the two vessels into parallel. *This should do it*, thought Mackey. But to everyone's astonishment on board *Mont Blanc*, the *Imo* suddenly tooted three abrupt blasts, indicating its engines were now full speed astern.

What happened next was no doubt Captain Le Médec and Pilot Mackey's worst nightmare. Despite the *Mont Blanc*'s engines now being full speed astern to get to the other side of the harbour, the *Imo* was still propelling forward. A collision between the two vessels was now unavoidable.

The *Imo*, complete with its hanging anchor, struck the bow of *Mont Blanc* and penetrated three metres into the ship's metal prow near the waterline. While it missed the TNT in the second hold, the first hold—with its barrels of picric acid and drums of benzol—was damaged. *Imo* immediately began to disengage. While backing out, the loud sound of metal grinding and scraping could be heard. Sparks flew near the dry acid and some of the benzol barrels had ruptured and were leaking. Small fires quickly broke out on the *Mont Blanc* and black smoke billowed. Suddenly, the forward deck burst into flame and the *Mont Blanc* began drifting helplessly towards Pier 6 on the Richmond shore.

CHAPTER 8

THE EXPLOSION

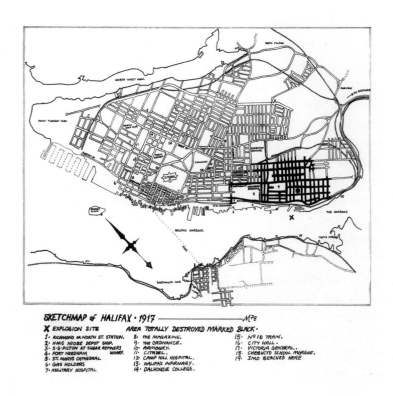

SKETCHMAP of HALIFAX · 1917 ————————— M⁷⁸

X EXPLOSION SITE   AREA TOTALLY DESTROYED MARKED BLACK ·

1· RICHMOND or NORTH ST. STATION.   8· THE MAGAZINE.   15· Nº 10 TRAIN.
2· H·M·S· NIOBE DEPOT SHIP.   9· THE ORDNANCE.   16· CITY HALL.
3· S·S·PICTON AT SUGAR REFINERS   10· ARMOURY.   17· VICTORIA GENERAL.
4· FORT NEEDHAM   WHARF.   11· CITADEL.   18· CHEBUCTO SCHOOL MORGUE.
5· ST. MARYS CATHEDRAL.   12· CAMP HILL HOSPITAL.   19· IMO BEACHED HERE
6· GAS HOLDERS   13· HALIFAX INFIRMARY.
7· MILITARY HOSPITAL   14· DALHOUSIE COLLEGE.

Sketchmap of Halifax with devastated north end area marked in bold.

VERY FEW PEOPLE IN THE harbour knew what *Mont Blanc* had on board. For the next nineteen minutes, a number of unsuccessful attempts were made to put the fire out. Throughout the harbour, and especially in Richmond, people gathered and watched in amazement as flames shot far up into the air. On board *Mont Blanc,* Captain Le Médec and Pilot Mackey had few options. Unable to contain the fire or sink the vessel, Le Médec turned his attention to saving his crew. Ignoring small craft coming alongside offering to help and fully expecting the vessel to immediately explode, Le Médec yelled, "Abandon ship!" Within seconds, the two lifeboats were in the water and the men were on ropes and ladders, securing their places while grabbing oars. Soon all were accounted for except the chief engineer. But confusion took hold as Le Médec became reluctant to leave his ship.

Finally, the chief engineer was located and the first officer was able to convince the captain to leave. The crew were then seen furiously rowing the two lifeboats towards the Dartmouth shore. Upon landing near Turtle Grove, a quick headcount was taken, and the entire crew, including Pilot Mackey, ran for shelter in the woods, yelling to anyone who would listen to take cover.

One person who did listen was a young Mi'kmaw boy named William Paul. When a terror-stricken man yelled to the boy to run, a ship was going to explode, Paul saw the fear in the man's eyes and ran back to his village telling everyone to run away, an explosion was coming. William's mother was not convinced of the danger and even as William began to argue with his mother, it was four minutes past nine—and already too late.

Aboard the *Highflyer,* Captain H. N. Garnett noticed the fire and sent a whaler with a crew to see what could be done to put it out and keep *Mont Blanc* from running into the Richmond pier. Captain Brannan also sailed the *Stella Maris* back to the *Mont Blanc* after securing his scows, but by now the burning vessel had reached Pier 6 and the wooden dock was on fire. The pinnace—light rowboat—from *Niobe* was dispatched as well, and since it became obvious the fire could not be put out, a cable was attached to *Mont Blanc* with the hopes of towing the burning ship back out into the harbour. But the cable was judged too weak so a larger cable was found and secured to the burning freighter. No one fighting the *Mont Blanc* fire knew that high explosives were aboard and with flames shooting thirty metres into the air, little could be done to bring the inferno under control.

After the collision, the *Imo* seemed to be still seaworthy. Those aboard watched as the crew of *Mont Blanc* mysteriously abandoned their burning ship. Were they jumping ship because they thought the *Mont Blanc* might sink? Perhaps it was only a gasoline fire that would eventually burn out thought Captain From, unaware of the freighter's real cargo. The *Imo*'s crew also mistakenly assumed that if munitions were aboard, a red flag would be flying. Pilot Hayes and Captain From decided to return the *Imo* to the Bedford Basin but had difficulty turning around in the crowded harbour and slowly headed toward the open ocean instead. Yet something was amiss on board the *Imo*—eyewitness accounts claimed the vessel drifted aimlessly until the explosion drove it onto a Dartmouth beach.

Lieutenant James Murray was aboard the harbour tug *Hilford* that morning since he worked for the Royal Navy coordinating the convoy office with the various merchant ships gathered in the basin. Over thirty merchant vessels were in the harbour and a convoy was preparing to leave Halifax the next day. Murray, along with his superior, convoy chief Rear Admiral Chambers, might have been told by New York of the incoming munitions ships that was expecting to join an armed procession overseas. Whether he actually knew of the deadly mix of high explosives is unclear. Yet upon seeing the smoking freighter, Murray sped to the scene and may have heard Mackey's warning from the lifeboat. Regardless, Murray was certainly aware of an imminent threat. He rushed to Pier 9, sending a sailor to warn the Richmond Railway office near the pier.

Inside the rail terminal, clerk William Lovett and dispatcher Vincent Coleman were told to run for cover by a panic-stricken sailor. Lovett immediately phoned his head office and rushed out the door, followed by Coleman. But Vincent Coleman turned around and went back inside, remembering a passenger train was due in Halifax shortly. He sent out one final dispatch to warn the oncoming train: "Munitions ship on fire. Making for Pier 21. Goodbye." Within seconds of transmitting the telegraph message, Vincent Coleman was dead, and while his heroic effort to warn trains of an impending explosion was not successful, his actions were deemed courageous and in 2017, Halifax announced a new harbour ferry would be named in his honour. Yet Coleman's message did get out and may have been picked up by other railway operators since throughout eastern North America, telegrams were relayed with the message that Halifax had been hit with a terrific explosion.

Halifax Railroad Station, in which 60 Persons were killed by falling roof.
—Copyright Underwood & Underwood, N.Y.

Intercolonial Railway Station destroyed by the blast, December, 1917. The trusses and glass roof were blown apart.

Meanwhile Frederick Wyatt, on his way to the dockyard and knowing full well what was on board the burning ship, was finally told of the collision. He became worried as he ordered up a motorboat and ran down to the docks to assess the situation. With *Mont Blanc* now resting up against the wooden pier, the fire had intensified amid the constant supply of explosions. Wyatt knew then it was hopeless: the munitions ship would soon explode. Indeed, his motorboat never did arrive.

The fireworks were dazzling. Some of the nearby ships were being rocked by the blasts as bits of cargo blew up, and the innocent citizens of Halifax and Dartmouth were crowding the harbour's shores in awe of the spectacle. Other people were watching through their windows at home and numerous sailors plus waterfront workers were also glued to the scene of the fiery ship.

As *Mont Blanc* burned, the fire alarm rang at the West Street Fire Engine House. Halifax's only motorized fire pumper, *Patricia*, was dispatched. The driver was Billy Wells and along with a fire crew—Chief Edward Condon followed in his 1911 McLaughlin Buick—they turned the siren on, headed toward the water, and along Campbell Road to Pier 6.

At precisely 9:04:34 a.m., the *Mont Blanc* was blown to pieces.

The power of the explosion was unprecedented: the largest human-made eruption to that time, second only today to Hiroshima. The toxic combination of almost three thousand tons of explosives triggered the most deadly bomb ever seen in human history. A massive fireball rose above the *Mont Blanc* and homes nearby were instantly flattened. Glass shattered into flying slivers cutting through everything including human eyes, faces, and chests.

A giant cloud of smoke and flames flashed high into the sky—the *Mont Blanc* was no more. A few surviving pieces of the ship were tossed across the peninsula like toys. A barrel of one of the guns weighting 544 kilograms landed over three kilometres away at Albro Lake in Dartmouth, and an anchor shaft weighting 517 kilograms landed five kilometres away at Armdale on Halifax's

Northwest Arm. Many people reported hearing two blasts since the sound coming through the ground would have been faster than what travelled through the air.

Windows broke over 80 kilometres away. In Sydney, Cape Breton, 430 kilometres to the northeast, residents could feel the shock of the blast. In the Halifax Harbour and in the north-end neighbourhood of Richmond, destruction was immense: almost 2,000 people were killed, 9,000 were injured, 6,000 were left homeless, and 25,000 reported damaged homes. For some time, perhaps up to ten minutes, it rained a mixture of oily grunge and shrapnel, and pieces of hot metal—some large enough to kill or seriously injure—fell through roofs and landed on decks of ships.

On the *Middleham Castle*, off the Graving Dock, massive boulders were seen lying on the deck as the young apprentice Jack Tappen and two other sailors picked themselves up after landing on a pile of bodies. Amid the carnage, the young men managed to get ashore but what they encountered in Richmond was much worse.

Third officer aboard the *Middleham Castle*, Charles Mayers, recalled hearing cries from his fellow officers before he was tossed by the blast and spun through the air, falling to the ground almost a kilometre away on top of Fort Needham. Badly cut, Mayers was lucky to be alive—but had landed stark naked except for his boots. Some men gave him pants and a coat, and he remembered a young girl crying next to him.

Piers 6 through 9 were totally destroyed and a number of ships that managed to escape the direct blow of the blast were carried away in the ensuing tsunami. The surge rose as high as eighteen metres, flooding Windmill Road in Dartmouth and above Barrington Street in Richmond. After the wave passed, floating wreckage and bodies littered the water.

The community hit hardest from the giant wave—in fact there may have been two or even three waves—was Tufts Cove, including nearby Turtle Grove, where the tsunami sank and destroyed numerous small homes. There were many deaths. Of the forty families living at Tufts Cove, the relief committee reported that thirty-eight were rendered homeless and were in dire need of food in the days after the explosion. In fact, the food committee was so overwhelmed with requests that all three temporary food stations had to restrict their rations until American Red Cross workers arrived and undertook a door-to-door assessment of needs.

The *Curaca* at Pier 8 was ravaged, its stern heavily damaged before it was carried by the tsunami to Tufts Cove, where it sank with forty-five crewmembers lost. Captain Pack survived and had the terrible task of identifying the bodies of his crew. They were later buried in the Fairview Cemetery.

Collision of this Vessel the "S.S. Imo" with "Mont Blanc" Caused Great Halifax Disaster
—Copyright Underwood & Underwood, N.Y.

Imo beached on the Dartmouth shore, December, 1917. The vessel was hurled across the harbour and then swamped by a giant wave. Both Captain From and Pilot Hayes perished as well as five crewmembers while the survivors were rescued by the *Highflyer*.

The *Imo* was wrecked by the explosion and floated on a giant wave to the Dartmouth shore where it beached on its starboard side. Captain From and Pilot Hayes both perished in the explosion, as well as five other crewmembers. *Imo* survivors were evacuated after the *Highflyer* came alongside to rescue the sailors.

Tugboats and whalers that sought to help the burning *Mont Blanc* before it blew up did not fare well. On the *Stella Maris*, six of the twenty-four men survived but Captain Brannen did not; the severely damaged tug ran aground near Pier 6. No one from the *Niobe*'s pinnace survived but one crewmember of the *Highflyer*'s rowboat did. And the tug *Hilford* was taken by the tsunami and tossed up onto Pier 9. Lieutenant James Murray perished in the explosion while in the midst of calling the convoy office. Seven sailors on the *Calonne* lost their lives and numerous crew members on the *Picton* perished, as well as sixty-four longshoremen involved in the vessel's overhaul. Farther out in the harbour, the damaged *Highflyer* lost three British crew and reported fifteen wounded, while *Old Colony* and *Olympic* were anchored in the basin and received only minor damage. *Highflyer* was damaged and in no position to escort the next day's convoy and the departure was postponed until December 11. Another vessel in the harbour, HMS *Changuinola*, an armed merchant vessel under the command of Lieutenant Sidney W. Baker, was organizing a fire crew to approach the *Mont Blanc* when the ship exploded.

Undaunted, Baker landed a party of men at Pier 4 and reported to harbour command on the *Niobe*. The crew was dispatched to undertake rescue work in the hard-hit areas of Richmond where blocked roads, fires, and badly burned victims made it difficult to carry out rescue efforts. Nevertheless, Baker's company searched through the fallen debris and extracted bodies from the rubble. Eventually the rescue party was able to acquire two tugs and transport the survivors to the American hospital ship *Old Colony*. In reporting to his superiors on December 7, Lieutenant Baker explained that the rescue effort mainly involved "clearing debris and extracting bodies from ruins." But Baker privately admitted that without fire-fighting equipment, some victims, even families, had to be abandoned as houses crashed and quickly burned to the ground.

At Pier 4, many buildings were destroyed while the headquarters of the Canadian navy, *Niobe*, suffered major damages as red-hot metal, rocks, and other flying rubble caused destruction and fire on its decks. The fires were quickly put out, but the tsunami rocked the vessel further. In all, nineteen men aboard the ship were killed and near the vessel, the lives of two divers were in jeopardy. The men had entered the water to check concrete foundations just before the explosion and were being fed air by four men from manual pumps above the surface. Two of the pumpers died immediately from the blast and another was knocked out. Walter Critch and John Gammon were also helping out but the explosion left them unconscious. Fortunately they came to in time to see the divers tangled in the lines and struggling to breathe. Critch began to work a manual air pump while Gammon was able to straighten a line and help get the men, in their heavy underwater suits, up the ladder and onto the dock just before the giant surge swamped the pier.

After the heroic rescue, Gammon went searching for his wife and four children at his Union Street house in Richmond. Finding his house demolished, Gammon set out for St. Joseph's School, only to find the structure destroyed and a number of deceased children in the ruins. A neighbour then told Gammon she had seen his wife and children die in the explosion. Stunned, Gammon searched through the destruction unsuccessfully. The next day, two of his children were located, one having been taken in by a family, and the other found wandering aimlessly. Despite advertising in the December 8 *Evening Mail* for his wife and two remaining children, Gammon got no response. But the next day, John Gammon stumbled across his semi-conscious wife, Maud, in the hospital. The family's two other children were never found.

Charles Duggan operated a motorized ferry, the *Grace Darling*, transporting workers from Dartmouth across to the factories in north-end Halifax. Duggan's older brother, Billy, was a champion rower and much of the Duggans' extended family lived on Campbell Road. After the collision, Charles Duggan approached the abandoned *Mont Blanc* in the *Grace Darling*, thinking he could help. He quickly saw the fire was too intense and he crossed over to Dartmouth.

As he approached Tufts Cove, the explosion occurred and the tsunami engulfed Duggan's ferry and drove him to the bottom of the harbour. He lost consciousness as a second wave picked him up and deposited him in a field near the French Cable Wharf. Six days later, Duggan told the *Daily Echo* that first there was "a cloud of smoke [that] must have been two hundred feet in the air. Then came the most appalling crash I have ever heard, and my boat went under my feet as if some supernatural power had stolen her from me while I myself was thrown into the harbour."

When Charles Duggan came to, his clothes were missing except for his underwear. His prized possession, the *Grace Darling*, was shattered into tiny pieces. He tried to walk back to Richmond where his wife, Reta, and their infant son were, but he was too unsteady. As he slowly made his way towards Windmill Road he was shocked to see the Oland Brewery in ruins and the big Cordage Company smokestack completely gone. The Mi'kmaw village at Turtle Grove was on fire and everywhere he looked houses, churches, and buildings of all sorts had vanished or were half destroyed. He could not make sense of it. Was it a bad dream or had the Germans really destroyed everything? He managed to limp, and at times crawl, to Baxter's store but found the half-wrecked building empty and the owner dead.

Next Charles set out toward the ferry terminal, passing more destruction. On Queen Street, a Dr. Dickson had dragged his dining room out into his yard, covered it with a white cloth, and was attending to his wounded patients. Despite some broken windows and other minor damages, the ferry was still operating and would continue to take passengers back and forth across the harbour throughout the day—at no charge. And from the deck of the ferry, Charles could see that the worst damage by far was in Richmond. But soldiers on guard at North Street turned him back and he ended up staying with relatives in the west end. The next day he and his brother set out again in search of their families.

The tragedy for Charles and his brother Billy was unimaginable. In all, over fifty Duggan relatives were gone. Confusion ran rampant in the local newspapers—dubious identification lists were published daily—and only added to their grief. Billy, at sea aboard the minesweeper *P. V. VII* during the disaster, came home to find numerous family members in the Chebucto mortuary. He lost his mother, father, brother, sister, and even one of his own children. Yet he found his seriously injured wife, Lottie, and four of their five children alive in Camp Hill Hospital. Their youngest child was missing and they eventually concluded that the infant had perished in the house fire. Lottie would suffer headaches the rest of her life from glass that had been lodged in her skull. For many years, glass and other debris were found and removed from her head.

The homes of both brothers were destroyed but Charles suffered a terrible ordeal, searching the morgue before finally finding his dead wife clutching their baby beneath the family's wrecked home. It was a terrible time for the Duggan brothers. Charles received six hundred dollars compensation for the loss of his ferry and six weeks later, Billy and his five-member family were still living with twelve relatives in a small house west of Richmond. And the tragedy that struck the Duggan family was not unique. The Jackson family of Richmond lost forty-six members with another nineteen seriously injured. Their appalling story—one family's tragedy—became the basis for the book *Too Many To Mourn*.

Turtle Grove, Mi'kmaq encampment near Dartmouth, c.1900. W. L. Bishop photo.

CHAPTER 9

DESTRUCTION

IN THE WOODS BEHIND TURTLE Grove, the crew of the *Mont Blanc* were bloodied and bruised, including Pilot Mackey and Captain Le Médec, who had both been knocked out by a fallen tree. One crewmember, gunner Yves Gueguiner, had been hit with a large piece of metal and was bleeding badly. The men were able to get him help but he later passed away. Francis Mackey managed to make his way to the Dartmouth waterfront, where he boarded the ferry and crossed back to Halifax.

But at Turtle Grove, the situation was desperate. Chief Lonecloud was away in Kentville at the time of the explosion and rather than running for cover as William Paul had insisted, many band members had gone to the beach to watch the fireworks. Hot metal rained down on the shore and woods, where fire destroyed seven homes. Of the thirty-eight known band members, nine were killed. Jerry Lonecloud's daughter Rosie was pinned under timbers and eventually died. William Paul's mother, who was pregnant at the time, woke up after the explosion to the sound of a baby crying. Despite bodies lying nearby, Mrs. Paul began to pull at a pile of wood; the cries got louder. Finally she uncovered part of her stove that was still burning. On top of the hot coals lay her youngest child, baby Madeline, screaming in pain but still alive.

Mrs. Paul then found her son Blair alive but seriously injured. She got on her knees to pray for William when suddenly he walked out of the woods, unharmed. A number of Turtle Grove survivors were reported to have spent time in

Mrs. Newill, and Jerry Lonecloud on right. Mrs. Lonecloud may be the person seated. This 1913 photo was possibly taken in Shubenacadie.

the shelter at Imperial Oil and baby Madeline would remain in hospital for over a year with serious burns all over her body.

The tragedy hit the little community so hard that many surviving families drifted away and resettled near Shubenacadie. Yet both the Nivens and Lonecloud families remained at the grove and today, Nivens Avenue still runs from Windmill Road down to the harbour.

The Dartmouth Relief Committee provided Turtle Grove with some financial assistance but the school was completely destroyed and never rebuilt. Today, Turtle Grove is home to many apartment buildings while three huge power funnels dominate the skyline. Nearby an old military housing complex called Shannon Park is being transformed into a modern housing and retail complex with participation from the Mi'kmaw community.

RICHMOND

While significant destruction had occurred throughout the harbour and in Dartmouth, Halifax's north end—around Richmond—suffered the most damage by far. For about two square kilometres, anything standing was utterly destroyed. Many people died from flying window glass or getting trapped in burning buildings.

Acting dockyard superintendent Fred Pasco had been upstairs in his house facing the window when the blast occurred. Cuts to his face and body from flying glass made it almost impossible for him to see yet he staggered outside. He joined patrol Captain Walter Hose, setting up a make-

Gottingen Street, December 1917. The day after the explosion, passes were issued for authorization to enter Richmond.

shift station on the dockyard where soldiers and ships' companies could report for duty. While the dockyard itself was in shambles, soldiers were told to fan out through Richmond and assist the needy. This quick thinking did much to kick-start the relief effort.

Death and destruction were everywhere. The huge Acadia Sugar Refinery, between Hanover and Young Streets, was destroyed resulting in many deaths including those who had climbed on top of the structure to watch the *Mont Blanc* burn. The destruction and chaos was so great that the body of mechanical superintendent Vincent Pattison wasn't found amid the wreckage until the following spring. All four Richmond churches were flattened and about nine hundred congregation members were all instantly killed. Schools were wrecked and hundreds of children perished while some were blinded from the flying glass. Every major business—including Hillis & Sons Foundry, the Richmond Printing Company, and the North Street Railway Station—was either

Mi'kmaw school at Tufts Cove after the explosion, December 1917. The principal, George Richardson, was killed on his way to school while the Mi'kmaw children were waiting in the building. Some children were killed and at least seven homes were destroyed. The school was never rebuilt.

demolished or severely damaged. The grand old North Street Station handled passenger service for the Intercolonial Railway. Sixty employees died as the station's glass roof collapsed and both rails and cars were blasted into the harbour. Eventually the King Edward Hotel next door was repaired but the station was never rebuilt, and railway service moved to the city's south end.

The *Patricia* fire engine was battered and wrecked and gone were Chief Condon, his deputy, and the engine's crew—all except driver Billy Wells, who was left standing without clothes and with a badly injured right arm that would never heal properly. In all, nine firefighters were killed on duty on December 6 but the *Patricia* was rebuilt and remained in service until 1942. An estimated fifty horses perished in the north end streets, and fires from flying metal and overturned stoves burned down whatever was wooden and still half-standing.

Cut and maimed people, many in a zombie-like state of shock, roamed the streets searching for loved ones when a sudden call went out to abandon the north end as a second blast was imminent. The fear centered on the Wellington Barracks where the garrison magazine was fuming after coal sparks had escaped from the furnace room. Upon inspecting the wide-open munitions shed, Lieutenant C. A. McLennan discovered a large steel plate from the *Mont Blanc* had been blown into the building, making the magazine a potential powder keg.

People, including some soldiers, began to run to safer ground to the west but most ended up on the Commons behind Citadel Hill. The scene was sheer pandemonium amid the dead, dying, and badly injured. Meanwhile Lieutenant McLennan, along with soldiers from Company B, acted quickly and bravely by separating the fuel from the munitions boxes, dragging the combustibles outside onto the lawn. Even after the flames were put out by dousing water on the smouldering ammunition, panic remained in the north end as clouds of smoke and steam appeared above the barracks. By about 2:00 P.M., the north end was declared safe thanks to McLennan's soldiers painstakingly removing smoking coal and ammunition from the magazine.

Fourteen-year-old Barbara Orr and her family lived in a new house on Albert Street just minutes from the Richmond Printing Company, her father's business. She attended Grove Presbyterian Church and Richmond School. On the morning of December 6, though, Barbara and her siblings were home; her brothers and sisters had been quarantined with measles. The fiery ship in the harbour caused great excitement among the children and despite her brother claiming to know the vessel was an ammunitions ship, their mother doubted the ship would explode and gave permission for the children to go outdoors. Barbara headed down the hill to visit her friend but partway down, she stopped and watched as balls of flames began to burst upwards. A loud *boom* and suddenly she was floating through the air, almost dreamlike. She flew up the hill about half a kilometre and landed at the top of Fort Needham.

Barbara remembered hearing people saying Germans had bombed the harbour, causing the explosion. She was unable to walk due to her injured foot and leg, and crawled down to Gottingen Street where she thought she might be able to find help. Barbara was able to make it safely to her aunt's damaged house on Gottingen Street. But Barbara's aunt did not recognize her at first—Barbara's bright red hair was covered in black soot. When asked about her family, Barbara replied, "They are all gone."

She didn't know it at the time, but she was right; she lost her mother, father, and brothers and sisters.

Barbara's father and uncle were among the thirty employees at Richmond Printing who perished in the explosion. Transported on a horse-drawn fish truck, Barbara was later taken to the Camp Hill Hospital along with an estimated 1,400 others admitted that day. While she eventually recovered from her injuries, it was months before she could walk without pain and a black scar would remain on her face.

Ten-year-old Jean Hunter, a classmate of Barbara's at Richmond School, ended up living in a boxcar with her family for twelve days after their home on Agricola Street was badly damaged. With an improvised bathroom and curtain at one end, the Hunters found old beds, dishes, and a stove, and managed to make the best of it. Fortunately their home was one of the first to be rebuilt by the reconstruction committee. Relief funds also paid for the Hunters' replacement furniture.

Nineteen-year-old Lillian Atkins had only been working at the Dominion Textiles Factory for a few weeks. She had moved to Halifax from Yarmouth and was living in a boarding house. Her job involved looking after one of the spinning machines that churned out cotton fabrics. Although it was only nine o'clock in the morning on December 6, the huge stone building at the corner of Young and Robie Streets was already humming. Less than five minutes later,

Atkins was cut and bleeding, lying on the third floor with the stone walls cracked and all the windows blown out. Pieces of concrete and large machines had crashed through the cotton factory, killing and maiming employees. Bleeding from her face and arm, Lillian was able to stand and walk. The floors were slippery with

Dominion Textile Limited on Robie Street before the explosion.

blood, and people began screaming throughout the ruins. Bales of cotton had caught fire and Lillian knew she had to somehow get out of the building.

She made it to the ground floor and out on to Robie Street, where she sat on the sidewalk until two soldiers came by offering her a warm greatcoat and help to get home. When they arrived at her boarding house, though, they found it completely destroyed. The soldiers escorted Lillian to the Wellington Barracks. Amid the damaged barracks, and now barely able to walk, Lillian was able to find shelter and was later sent to Camp Hill Hospital. She eventually received treatment but also assisted doctors treating other injured people before she headed home to safety on a Yarmouth-bound train.

Joe Glube lived with his family on Gottingen Street and owned a tobacco and stationery store. The twenty-one-year old had somehow been sleeping during the explosion itself and woke to a great commotion. The house, which was near North Street, had been hit hard. When news of a potential second blast reached them, Glube and his family began walking to the Commons. It was cold and Joe's mother had left behind her new fur coat, so Joe returned to the house to get it. Unable to relocate his family back at the Commons and not really knowing the damage sustained in the north end, Joe went to check on his store on Barrington Street near

Ruins of the textile factory with the Exhibition Building in the background.

City Hall. The building was standing but the glass had been blown out. As Glube started to board up the smashed windows, Deputy Mayor Colwell began appealing for help through a megaphone, asking for donations of automobiles to transport supplies to the city's north end.

Joe fired up his old Model-T Ford and drove to the Armoury where he was loaded up with milk, blankets, and other emergency items. The young merchant then drove to Richmond and was shocked to see the destruction, having to take charge at one point and clear dead bodies from the road in order to reach the needy. Joe was able to transport the injured to hospitals and spent the day going back and forth from Richmond to the south end.

Joe and his family couldn't return to their smashed-in house, but did have relatives nearby to stay with. Joe reported to the Armouries again the next day despite a raging blizzard. The chaos was summed up in a single *Halifax Herald* headline: HALIFAX WRECKED. That day, December 7, Joe ended up assisting Dr.

Philip Gough who was going door to door and patching people up. He also continued to deliver the seriously wounded to hospitals. He went on to have a successful career as a Halifax home furnishing merchant.

Besides gas and electricity, food, clean water, and milk had disappeared in Richmond. Feeding survivors became paramount. By noon, a cooking brigade had formed, but part of the problem was making sure the food was free of glass chips. Restaurants pitched in to help. The Green Lantern on Barrington Street was perhaps the best-known eatery in the city. Besides giving away its food, the Green Lantern assisted the clothing committee by organizing a collection of used clothing and footwear. It was said that a line of people donating clothing stretched one way down Barrington Street, and another line went the other way with victims graciously accepting the warm clothes and boots.

One particularly poignant account of the explosion came from a fourteen-year-old boy who would go on to become one of Nova Scotia's greatest writers. Thomas Raddall was a Grade 9 student at the two-storey brick Chebucto School in Halifax's west end. At school that morning, he experienced two quite distinct shocks: the first felt like an earthquake, and the second more like a strong air blast, which left him concussed, affecting him for the rest of his life. Raddall lived close to his school and got home to discover his mother deeply cut in the chest from exploding glass and blaming the Germans for shelling her city.

Ellen Raddall was patched up at Camp Hill and she and her children—Raddall's father was serving overseas—spent much of the day repairing their broken house. That evening Raddall was summoned back to Chebucto School by some soldiers who were in search of a place to establish a central morgue. Raddall led the soldiers into the basement where, after striking a match, the sergeant declared, "Hold a thousand, easy."

The men behind the idea of one central morgue were Alderman R. B. Colwell and former mayor Robert MacIlreith, the latter a

The Royal Naval College of Canada was established in 1911 in the old Naval Hospital at the north end of the dockyard. At the time of the explosion, thirty-eight cadets were in residence but the college was so badly damaged that the cadets were transferred to Kingston until the college was permanently moved to Esquimalt, B.C.

key member of the relief committee charged with coordinating the overall operation. MacIlreith was mayor when the *Titanic* sank five years earlier and knew first-hand the value of having one central area to identify and organize the deceased. Recognizing and burying the dead had become a major task when the more than two hundred bodies from the giant liner arrived in Halifax. Now the Halifax Explosion loomed large: the job was going to entail processing and burying thousands of victims. Arthur Barnstead was actually appointed chairman of the mortuary committee— his father had undertaken the same duties after the *Titanic* disaster.

Before long, wagons pulled up to the Chebucto School with bodies. The next day, December 7, the wagons formed a procession and another line formed of survivors attempting to identify their loved ones. Living nearby, the young Raddall later wrote in his autobiography, *In My Time*, that the whole mortuary in the school basement was filled with bodies and resembled Madame Tussaud's Chamber of Horrors. The army sergeant had been right: a total of 1,200 corpses were held at the Chebucto School.

A great deal of the dead were identified by their families and taken away for burial. There were those who were mutilated or scorched so badly that they were unrecognizable; they were placed in coffins for a mass funeral service on December 17 in front of the

Public funeral of unidentified dead at Chebucto School, December 17, 1917.

school. In total, there were ninety-five unidentified victims. Over three thousand people attended the service and the coffins were supposed to be buried in graves at Fairview, but as unknown dead, they were instead buried in a mass potter's field grave on Bayers Road.

Until January 11 when the search for victims was officially called off, soldiers continued to locate bodies among the destruction and sent the bodies—often simply charred remains—to the Chebucto morgue. The job of identifying remains or even partial remains became increasingly difficult as the mortuary staff often had little to work with. In fact, information management was the worst headache for the relief committee. Relatives and friends would search high and low for tips or pieces of information about the missing, including such grisly details published in the newspapers as:

"No 441 Male. Age about 40 years. Brown hair, sandy moustache. Fleece lined underwear. Two cotton shirts. Grey heavy wool socks, striped grey pants."

"No. C.581. Charred remains taken from 41 North Albert Street, brought in old tin trunk."

"Baby: An unknown baby boy about seven months old, brown eyes and hair and uninjured. Picked up on Herring Cove Road on the day of the explosion now at the Infants' Home."

And even more shocking were some of the desperate advertisements that appeared in the *Halifax Herald, Morning Chronicle,* and *Evening Mail* including: "Would the soldier who rescued baby from unconscious woman's arms on Longard Road the morning of the explosion return baby to its parents, 9 Longard Road."

Despite being close to Richmond, Africville got off relatively light in the explosion. The community faced the Bedford Basin and between the village and the Narrows, a rocky headland took much of the force of the blast. Nevertheless, ten residents died as doors and windows were blown apart just like in other parts of the city. Later on, relief investigators incorrectly decided that Africville had suffered only minor damages and just ten percent of residents' losses would be covered, rather than the twenty percent other Haligonians received.

Women walking from Africville towards Halifax, on Campbell Road near Hanover Street. The community suffered less damage than Richmond but five residents died, including a woman identified as Esther Roan. She reportedly died from injuries sustained while walking into work. The day of the explosion, a number of men from the village went into Richmond to help with the relief effort.

CHAPTER 10

RESCUE AND RELIEF

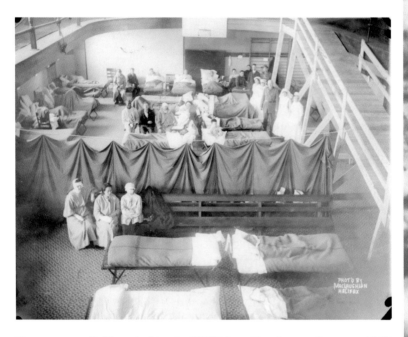

Emergency relief hospital in the YMCA on Barrington Street, c.1917.
One of the volunteers is Lola Henry and the building is now the Pacific
Building located at 1541 Barrington Street.

LIKE MOST CITIES AT THE time, Halifax had neither public
safety organizations nor much in the way of social services.
The fire department had suffered heavy fatalities and the city's
police department, with less than fifty men for a city of fifty

thousand, was also short-staffed. Four public hospitals had been established: the Victoria General, the Children's Hospital, the Nova Scotia Hospital for Infectious Diseases in Dartmouth, and a smaller hospital for infectious diseases near Africville. There were also seven small private hospitals as well as military hospitals and convalescent facilities on Cogswell Street, Rockhead Prison, and Pine Hill. There were five undertakers between Halifax and Dartmouth. Due to the rapid rise in the war wounded returning to Halifax, Admiralty House had also been turned into a military hospital.

Within a short time, all facilities were quickly overrun as severely injured citizens were admitted or simply showed up, waiting in line for assistance. While every building still standing needed some sort of repair, virtually every sizeable building not shattered was put to use as a medical facility, supply depot, or homeless shelter. By Christmastime, the medical relief committee had opened many additional temporary facilities providing beds for about one thousand people.

One resource that Halifax had depended upon since its foundation proved to be so valuable that without it, the fallout from the explosion would have been much worse. By noon on December 6— mere hours after the explosion— Lieutenant Governor MacCallum Grant, chairman of the newly established relief committee, had granted the military and naval establishments full emergency powers. The Halifax Relief Committee had been hastily formed at city hall, where the clock in the north tower had stopped just seconds before 9:05 A.M. (The clock was never repaired and to this day remains frozen in time.)

To kick-start the relief effort, Halifax Police Chief Frank Hanrahan and Deputy Mayor Henry Colwell immediately called Colonel W. E. Thompson at military headquarters on Spring Garden Road. Colonel Thompson reported directly to Canada's top military authority in Halifax, Major-General Thomas Benson. Special authority was granted to the military and several committees were struck: emergency shelter, food, transportation, medical, finance, and mortuary. Very quickly, those sailors and soldiers not injured fanned out across the north end to help. In a number of burning homes, they came across people trapped and desperate for assistance. Without any identification, numerous babies were found alone and rushed to the nearest hospital.

Besides clearing streets of debris and human and animal remains, military personnel were authorized to seize automobiles to transport the injured to hospitals and the homeless to makeshift shelters. While martial law was never officially declared, some cars were seized by force, especially by the 63rd Halifax Rifles at the intersection of North Park and Cunard streets. Colonel Thompson's orders had been clear: "Wherever you want a car or a team, stop and take it." Drivers not willing to co-operate were thrown out of their cars. By evening, the committee had commandeered almost three hundred automobiles.

Children getting food from a relief station, December 1917. This photo was later released as a tinted postcard by H. H. Marshall.

Preparing to leave for the war in Europe, the British Expeditionary Force had been quartered at the Halifax Armoury. Though shaken, the structure remained standing and was later used as a food-storage depot. The expeditionary force of about 150 formed into squads and sifted through the wreckage to find and transport injured citizens to safety. They were invaluable; as wartime soldiers, their training was exactly what a devastated Halifax and Dartmouth needed. That first night, as the freezing cold set in, tents with mattresses and blankets were set up on the Commons for civilians. Many soldiers slept in them instead, offering their heated military quarters to the homeless and injured.

The other essential service the military provided was patrolling the streets and guarding the abandoned and wrecked homes due to looting. An official permission slip called a "Pass for Devastated Area" signed by Chief of Police Franck Hanrahan was issued for entry into Richmond. Soldiers stood guard at key entry points and also patrolled the devastated neighbourhood on horseback. In some cases, residents were not allowed to return to their wrecked homes without official permission.

Naval assistance was also integral to the relief effort. The American hospital ship *Old Colony* sent one hundred sailors to shore to assist any way they could. They returned with two hundred gravely injured victims, of which twenty-five would die from their wounds. The day after the explosion the cruiser HMS *Isis* arrived in Halifax Harbour providing fresh sailors to relieve the exhausted search and rescue operators. And the USS *Tacoma* and USS *Von Steuben*, both cruising off Nova Scotia, also came into port to offer assistance. *Von Steuben* alone provided 250 sailors eager to assist.

DARTMOUTH

In parts of Dartmouth, especially in the city's north end, the situation was equally bleak. Hardly a building north of Dawson

Street was left standing. The roof was gone from the big Consumer Cordage factory, while every north-end school and church was damaged. The skating rink and light tower at the corner of Windmill and Wyse Roads were both destroyed. Even parts of the Starr Manufacturing Company were damaged.

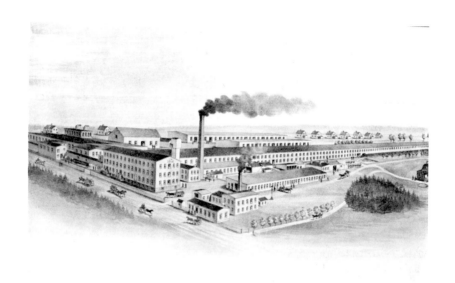

Consumers Cordage Company, Limited, North Dartmouth. Both the main ropeworks building and many of the employees' homes were damaged in the explosion. The roof and windows were blown out while both manager Leo Graham and employee George Ferguson each lost one eye.

Individuals in north Dartmouth suffered greatly. Reverend J. A. MacGlashen of Stairs Presbyterian Church lost his home on Windmill Road, but he and his wife dragged mattresses out into his yard and cared for many people until proper medical aid arrived. Reverend MacGlashen also gave last rights to the young *Mont Blanc* sailor, Yves Gueguiner, who was the lone sailor aboard the munitions ship to die after he was struck by flying metal.

Seventeen-year-old Ian Forsyth was attending the Halifax Academy when the explosion ripped through the city. He returned to Dartmouth on the ferry, describing the scene in the harbour as a "dreamlike experience—death, destruction, and fire all around." His mother had suffered a serious chest wound and their house on Windmill Road was almost completely destroyed; the roof was gone and the contents of one bedroom were scattered on the ground. After salvaging what he could, Forsyth began driving a horse and wagon, delivering the wounded to the Nova Scotia Hospital in Woodside. In all, 250 people were admitted that day, while 162 houses were deemed ruined. Their residents were left homeless.

TELEGRAMS

While the Halifax rail line had been destroyed all the way out to Rockingham, the surviving railway workers did not stand idly by. Dominion Atlantic Railway (DAR) president George Graham had been in his own railway car near North Street when it was rocked by the explosion. As he moved out among the ruins, he witnessed almost four hundred railcars destroyed, telegraph lines down, and at least twenty-five of his own employees dead. He walked through the destruction to Rockingham and sent a telegram to DAR head-quarters in Kentville, requesting a relief train with doctors, nurses, medical supplies, trackmen, and engineers be rushed to Halifax: "Organize a relief train and send word to Wolfville and Windsor to round up all doctors, nurses, and Red Cross supplies possible to obtain. No time to explain details but list of casualties is enormous."

Graham's telegram got through to the Annapolis Valley and was among the first telegrams relayed to authorities in Boston. One person who saw the alarming message the morning of December 6 in Boston was Henry Endicott, a shoe manufacturer and chairman of the Massachusetts Committee on Public Safety.

Local Associated Press correspondent James Hickey also managed to send a telegram that morning. Cut and bruised, Hickey roamed the downtown streets in search of a still-operational wire service. The telegram offices at both the Canadian Pacific (CP) and Western Union railways were out of order, but the Halifax & Bermuda Cable Company was able to get a quick news dispatch out to the Associated Press via Havana, Cuba. The next day, Hickey's terse announcement that Halifax was in ruins was published in a number of North American newspapers.

W. A. Duff, assistant chief engineer of the Canadian Government Railway—the Intercolonial Railway had been merged with other government railways in 1917—also happened to be in Halifax that day. He managed to reach Rockingham and sent a telegram to regional headquarters in Moncton requesting medical and relief supplies. Duff's telegram reached Saint John, Ottawa, and Montreal. Over the next few days, relief trains were dispatched from each city.

RAILWAYS

While the rail lines from the North Street Station five kilometres out had been destroyed or covered with debris, the main line was up and running two days after the explosion. By Monday, December 10, full passenger service resumed.

Electricity, telephone, and gas were also back a few days later, yet the main problem was that much of Richmond was basically a desert without any buildings left standing. Streets were virtually impassable and blocked with debris.

As trains were being organized to bring aid into the stricken city, another train was being assembled to take the injured and homeless out of Halifax. The No.10 left Rockingham about one-thirty for Truro with refugees including many desperate children. Despite the medical help on board—Wolfville's Dr. Avery DeWitt and a nurse had jumped aboard at Windsor Junction—the sight of the injured disembarking in Truro shocked the townsfolk there. The only nourishment aboard the train was some Christmas cake in sealed tins. Many disfigured children—one completely blind and without parents—wandered off the train, and everyone was covered in black soot. Three children reportedly died en route. Most of the passengers were taken to hastily prepared shelters including the courthouse, fire hall, and the Williams Street School where medical treatment was provided. In the days and weeks ahead, the Truro Hospital also served as an important emergency facility for explosion victims.

Back in Halifax, more misery greeted Deputy Mayor Henry Colwell's son, Garnet, and Garnet's girlfriend, Gwen Westhaver. On a twenty-four-hour pass from the military, Lieutenant Garnet was scheduled to sail for France the next day. For his last evening in town, he had taken Gwen to the theatre on December 5. Saddened by his departure, Garnet tasted tears on Gwen's lips after kissing her goodnight. After the next morning's explosion, Garnet raced on his bicycle to her home on Veith Street—only to find the house flattened. After two days of searching, Garnet found Gwen's body in the Chebucto School Mortuary.

The first medical team to arrive in Halifax was a DAR relief train from Kentville. Other trains began to arrive later that day. Medical staff and engineers were forced to walk into Halifax from Rockingham due to the destroyed rail line. The military had managed to clear Barrington Street from Richmond to downtown. One Valley doctor walking to Camp Hill Hospital, Percy McGrath, recalled the horrible scene in Richmond of seeing bodies stacked like cordwood on both sides of the road. And upon arriving at Camp Hill, Dr. McGrath, accompanied by his wife, a nurse, was overwhelmed with critically injured patients.

Colonel McKelvey Bell was a thirty-nine-year-old surgeon and was head of all the military hospitals in Halifax. He had served in France but after being appointed the chairman of the medical

The Victoria School of Art and Design on Argyle Street surrounded with pine box coffins. Snow & Co., Undertakers are next door. The art school sustained some damage and was used to store coffins while the principal, Arthur Lismer, drew sketches of the disaster. Lismer, one of the Canadian Group of Seven artists, missed the train from Bedford on the day of the explosion, and escaped injury. Today the building is a popular seafood restaurant.

relief committee, he told a reporter that he had "never seen anything on the battlefield equal to the scenes of destruction witnessed in Halifax." With his overseas experience, McKelvey Bell was the ideal person to take charge of the medical function, yet he vastly underestimated the number of injured. He initially turned down an offer from Ottawa for more doctors on December 6, only to hastily send another telegram a few hours later requesting more medical staff, volunteers, and supplies. With explosion victims crowding the military hospitals, McKelvey Bell was faced with yet another problem: where would the incoming war wounded be housed? A large ship of injured soldiers from overseas was headed to Halifax. It was eventually decided to reroute it to another port.

Luckily Nova Scotia was home to a talented county doctor who also happened to be a New York-trained ophthalmologist. Dr. George Cox had established his medical practice in Pictou County, and on December 6, he was on the afternoon train to Halifax. After walking to the stricken city from Rockingham, Dr. Cox was assigned to the newly opened Camp Hill Hospital. But the chaos and sheer number of badly injured overwhelmed him.

The Armouries, Halifax, N.S.

The Armouries was built on North Park Street during the Boer War. Shaken by the explosion, it was not seriously damaged. It had become militia headquarters and housed the British Expeditionary Force during the explosion. As the major north-end food relief depot, its bread line often stretched back to Agricola Street.

Without any recognizable order, Dr. Cox simply began picking out the most seriously disfigured and went to work, mainly attempting to repair eye and face damage inflicted from flying glass and metal. He worked for twenty-four hours non-stop in his makeshift eye ward, slept for three, and went back to his patients. It was like nothing he had experienced before.

Victims continued to appear with glass and bones protruding from all manner of injuries, and he was forced to ration his chloroform. In one afternoon alone Dr. Cox detached twenty-five eyes, dropping them into a bucket that had to be emptied by mid-afternoon. George Cox worked for three days straight and had vivid memories of the Halifax Explosion for the rest of his life.

While the people of the Maritimes responded quickly to help victims of the explosion, residents of Massachusetts were also working hard, even though they didn't quite yet know the magnitude of the situation.

CHAPTER 11

MASSACHUSETTS RESPONSES

"MARITIME EXPRESS FAST IN THE SNOW ON FOLLEIGH MOUNTAIN, FEBRUARY 1905."

Maritime Express train buried in snow at Folly Mountain near Truro in February 1905. Near the same location, a similar snowstorm in December 1917 buried the Boston and Maine Railway relief train full of supplies and medical personnel.

LESS THAN TWO HOURS AFTER the explosion Henry Endicott, chairman of the Massachusetts Committee on Public Safety, along with businessman James Phelan, met with Massachusetts Governor Samuel McCall at the State House in Boston. After reading the DAR telegram, Governor McCall was determined to act, even though the actual needs were less than clear. He dispatched his own telegram to the Halifax mayor stating,

"Reports only fragmentary. Massachusetts ready to go the limit in rendering every assistance you may be in need of."

Despite not receiving a response—lines were still down—Governor McCall met with the Massachusetts Committee on Public Safety that same afternoon. The committee was the first such public emergency response group in North America, combining both government and private resources in case of major wartime disasters. One such calamity had just taken place with a war ally north of the border.

Attended by a large group of members, the committee felt the urge to act despite the trickle of information coming in from Halifax. William Brooks, Surgeon General of Massachusetts, proposed sending a train full of medical personnel and supplies that very evening, and Governor McCall heartily agreed. Abraham Ratshesky, a prominent Massachusetts banker and public safety member, was appointed commissioner of the Halifax relief expedition. That same evening, Ratshesky left on a Boston and Maine Railway train bound for Halifax with doctors, other medical personnel, and supplies, and John Moors, head of the Massachusetts Red Cross.

As the relief train sped north, the temperature dropped and heavy, damp snowflakes fell. Despite being given the right of way, the train had difficulty getting through. In Halifax a raging blizzard had descended, temporarily suspending the search-and-rescue effort. Ignoring the snowstorm, the Boston train raced through the night until huge drifts in Folly Mountain outside of Truro forced it to stop in its tracks. But locals came out with shovels after hearing of the train's purpose and destination and early on December 8, the relief train arrived in Halifax.

Within hours, the American relief team had been given the Bellevue Building on Spring Garden Road to use as its own hospital. Despite significant damage, military personnel rapidly fixed up the building and after only twelve hours in the city, American doctors were undertaking intricate surgeries. Sixty-six patients

Bellevue, December 1917. The American relief hospital was established in the Officers Club on Spring Garden Road near Queen Street. With the stars and stripes flying, the US relief workers are pictured here with the Nova Scotia Technical College in the background.

were admitted that first day. Eventually there were 120 American doctors working in Halifax and Dartmouth, dispensing medicine and tending to explosion victims.

Relief aid from Massachusetts did not stop with that single train. In addition to cash being raised, two ships full of supplies were also sent to Halifax. The *Calvin Austin* was full of winter clothing, food, medical supplies, 25,000 US Army blankets, and, most importantly, building materials (including 1,486 cases of highly sought-after glass to repair blown-out windows). The *Northland* also sailed from Boston with ten gas-powered trucks, chauffeurs, fuel, glass, cement, nails, second-hand clothing, boots, shoes, and

Pullman Car interior, c.1910. This car is configured for daytime coach seating but could be converted into full sleeping berths at night. Pullmans were used extensively for overnight travel by the Intercolonial Railway and would have been filled will medical personnel coming into Halifax the day after the explosion.

over two thousand packages of beaverboard, arriving in Halifax on December 13.

Trucks with big signs on the side reading *Massachusetts to Halifax* were seen about the city and were welcomed by cheering Haligonians. The people of Massachusetts also sent twenty-five skilled glass and putty glaziers, willing to train Nova Scotians in the craft of installing glass.

A freezing blizzard had descended on the stricken community the day after the explosion, and pneumonia was becoming a great concern. Requests were sent out to the American Red Cross for anti-pneumonia serum. Amazingly, on December 10, a relief train assembled by Red Cross officials left New York with enough serum to protect the most vulnerable. The same Red Cross also sent a full X-ray unit along with a skilled operator. As well, the Boston Symphony conducted a benefit concert featuring the famous soprano Nellie Melba. Other vital assistance that came from Massachusetts included medical social workers, who set up most of the medical services in dressing stations, homes, and temporary shelters.

Most discharged patients, many with serious burns and eye damage, still needed additional care and getting back to normal life was complex. This transition necessitated the new and

Massachusetts-Halifax Relief Committee's furniture warehouse for the distribution of furniture to residents of temporary housing, 1918. The state contributed $750,000 in goods and money to acquire furniture in New England that was able to enter Canada duty-free. Furniture was then given to explosion victims as they moved into their new homes.

emerging field of psychological counselling, and a number of local volunteers received training from the American social workers. By the time the Boston workers left Halifax at the end of January, a permanent group of local social workers had been hired to continue their vital work with the explosion victims, many of whom suffered what we now know as post-traumatic stress disorder (PTSD).

Support sent to Halifax from near and far was remarkable. In addition to supplies and personnel, Massachusetts also contributed a significant amount of cash—in fact many thought the Halifax Relief Commission should have been called the Massachusetts-Halifax Relief Commission, given all the state contributed to relief efforts. New York, Chicago, and other American cities also contributed funds, and in London, England, a subscription fund netted $600,000 for Halifax. The British government donated almost $5 million while the Australian government sent $250,000.

The Canadian government immediately sent $6 million and in total, contributed $18 million, almost half of overall funds collected. Other donors included King George V, the British Red Cross, and the *Mont Blanc*'s owner, Compagnie Générale Transatlantique. John Eaton, the president of Eaton's, Canada's major department store, arrived in Halifax to open a supply depot that dispensed household items and necessities free of charge.

By December 13, relief supplies and medical support were judged adequate enough that Abraham Ratshesky, head of the Massachusetts-Halifax Relief Committee, decided to return to Boston. He made an impassioned speech on the train platform thanking his fellow Bostonians and Haligonians for their diligent work in the face of the overwhelming tragedy. "I am proud of what my state has done, and sincerely trust, when your city is once more established on more normal lines, that Halifax will be a bigger and better city," Ratshesky said. He promised he would return to Halifax in January with newly donated funds to establish a free furniture warehouse. John Moors of the American Red Cross left five days after Ratshesky on December 18. The last American Red Cross officials left Halifax on January 15, satisfied the city could now manage on its own. The entire mission had cost the American Red Cross just under $20,000.

Nova Scotia Technical College. Built in 1911 on Spring Garden Road, the Technical College became home to a medical supply depot during the relief effort. For five days, three hundred women volunteers sewed everything from medical dressings to children's garments until supplies from outside agencies became adequate.

CHAPTER 12

A BITTER ELECTION

WHILE CAMPAIGNING IN THE DECEMBER federal "khaki election" of 1917, Prime Minister Robert Borden reported hearing a boom from the explosion in Charlottetown. Despite a crippling snowstorm, Borden rushed to Halifax, toured the destruction, and helped organize the recovery and financial response. Borden was especially helpful in working with the American Red Cross and Massachusetts medical officials. A former Halifax lawyer and local incumbent Member of Parliament (MP), Borden promised to deliver whatever federal support necessary. He came through with significant financial aid and assisted fundraising efforts throughout the Dominion and abroad.

Canadian War Publicity Poster—Your Chums are Fighting, Why aren't You? Borden's conscription law would divide the country, making the December 17, 1917, federal election the most violent political contest ever fought in Canada.

With war casualties at an all-time high, the 1917 federal election was one of the most vicious and bloody political contests ever fought in Canada. Borden, the leader of the Unionist Party, had evoked the divisive conscription law, which isolated Quebec by vilifying all those who resisted the draft. Borden also enacted legislation that allowed all overseas military personnel to vote as well as women favourable to conscription—wives, daughters, sisters, and mothers of men serving overseas. The next year, most women in Canada received the federal voting franchise.

While Borden won with a large majority in most of Canada, voting was postponed in Halifax and Dartmouth—as was the local conscription drive—due to the explosion. Later, the two local Liberal candidates resigned to allow the Unionist candidates to be declared unopposed winners.

But the election divided French and English Canadians for decades—violent anti-conscription riots were common in Quebec. A number of historians, including J. D. M. Stewart, have called 1917 perhaps the worst year in Canadian history. Not only in terms of casualties from the First World War, but also because of the most bitter, divisive election in the country's history.

CHAPTER 13

PROFITEERING

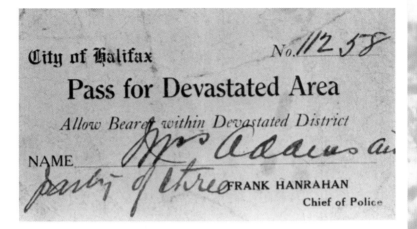

Pass for Devastated Area No. 11258. Passes like this were dispensed to control looters and speculators, allowing residents to entered Richmond to search for loved ones and personal effects.

ON DECEMBER 12, HALIFAX DEPUTY Mayor Henry Colwell issued a proclamation against profiteering—the process of overcharging for goods and services in short supply to make an excessive or unfair profit—warning that any instances would be dealt with severely. Widespread reports cited scavengers poking through the destruction and rummaging the Chebucto mortuary for anything of value to resell. Many occurrences of profiteering were reported, but few led to convictions. In one instance, a military officer working in the Chebucto School morgue stole cash from a mortuary bag and was put in jail; another soldier caught selling relief provisions was convicted of profiteering.

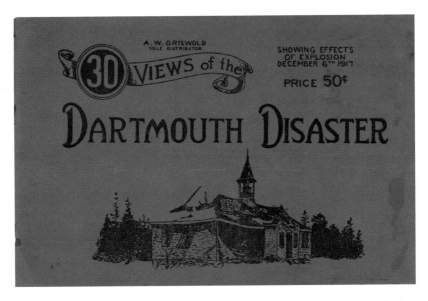

Views of the Dartmouth Disaster. Cover image of the booklet published in 1917 by A. W. Griswold and priced at fifty cents, featuring photos of the destruction and an introduction by A. C. Johnston, chairman of the Dartmouth Relief Committee.

To prevent incidents like these, armed patrols (consisting of militiamen, the Royal Navy, and later American sailors from *Tacoma* and *Von Steuben*) circulated the devastated sections, keeping an eye on things. One eyewitness account from Officer Richard Lee from HMS *Columbella* reported seeing a soldier on horseback carrying a rifle near the shattered sugar refinery—a looter nearby had been shot and hung in a doorway.

Despite this militaristic vigilance, landlords, shopkeepers, tradesmen, truckers, cabdrivers, and many others took advantage of the desperate situation by overcharging for their goods and services. Some unions would not allow their workers to work overtime without extra pay, and insisted on strict divisions of labour. This became so extreme that bricklayers would not allow other tradesmen to help repair chimneys for displaced families and so on.

With all the reconstruction, many new people came to Halifax looking for work. With the increase in population came an increase rise in crime, and that kept the police, already overtaxed with wartime issues, on their toes. One problem—prostitution—in the port city seemed to decline for a while as sex workers moved to better opportunities in larger cities. Yet prohibition was strictly re-enforced. Concerned citizens demanded bootleggers not prey upon the down-and-out, claiming the city could be overrun with drunkenness if prohibition was not promptly imposed.

Children on sleighs posing for the camera during the reconstruction, at the corner of Blowers and Grafton Streets, 1917 or 1918.

CHAPTER 14

CHILDREN OF THE EXPLOSION

WHILE SCHOOL-AGED CHILDREN WERE GENERALLY happy that school was cancelled from December until March, that didn't mean they hadn't suffered immensely from the disaster. Within days it became obvious that children presented unique problems for the relief committee. Orphaned, disabled, blind, homeless, misidentified, and missing children all created distinct challenges. On December 11, a special children's committee was created under the chairmanship of Ernest Blois, the provincial superintendent of neglected and delinquent children. The committee included judges, doctors, and teachers, as well as social workers from outside Halifax. An immediate priority was to reunite children with their parents, or relatives if the parents were deceased. Many fathers were away serving overseas and if the mother was killed or injured, children became dependants of the state.

At the time, orphanages were organized along religious lines and financed by churches and private funds. Protestant orphanages sought to acquire Protestant children and Catholic institutions followed the same policy. Adoptions were also structured according to religious affiliation. If a motherless family included a father working long hours, it was not uncommon for the father to pay an institution to board his young children.

Over four hundred letters from all over North America came into the committee with offers to adopt, often with very specific demands such as "good Scotch parentage" or "without physical deformities." But the children's committee was determined to keep the children in Nova Scotia if possible. Initially, Chairman Blois was tasked with locating and identifying missing children, repairing the children's institutions, and arranging for the long-term care and guardianship of homeless children. The need was substantial.

By the end of December, the children's committee had dealt with five hundred families and three times as many affected children. Two hundred children had been hospitalized and over fifty were blind or suffered serious eye injuries. Mothers and fathers reporting blindness or other serious injuries were also registered with the committee. Almost two hundred fatherless children were tallied and more than one hundred motherless children. Seventy children were immediately orphaned after the explosion, and while the need to place these children with foster parents or relatives was pressing, another eighty children could not been accounted for and were either missing, misidentified, or dead.

If both a child's parents had perished, the committee's preference was to try and place the orphans with relatives. Many children were given the option of picking where they might go. Fourteen-year-old Barbara Orr was able to choose from three families of relatives, and eventually decided to live with her Aunt Edna and Uncle William because they had children around her age.

By January, most of the missing children had still not been found and were added to the list of explosion victims. There were some happy moments as a few children were found, but the reality was small children were simply not easy to locate among the rubble. With the forty centimetres of heavy snow that fell on December 7, the search was made especially difficult. Yet searchers did manage to find one infant alive and without frostbite, nestled against a puppy.

One woman, the wife of a man named Private Benjamin Henneberry, had been found after having been buried for five hours near their apartment in the Flinn Block. But the next day, five of their children were still missing and Private Henneberry continued to dig through the debris. Thinking he could hear cries under the smoking ruins, he excitedly yelled to soldiers nearby for help. They found a girl about two years old under a stove.

The child was burned, but she had been protected from the worst of the fire by an ashpan that had fallen on her. Henneberry had assumed the grime-covered baby was his own, but in the Pine Hill Hospital days later, the child recognized Charlotte Liggins, who was with her daughter on a visit to the hospital. Despite *Olive Henneberry* being printed on the child's cot, Mrs. Liggins cried out, "That's a Liggins!" The child's family had also lived in an apartment in the Flinn Block, and she was properly identified as Annie Liggins and reunited with her aunt, since her mother and brother had died in the disaster (her father was still overseas). In all, forty-five residents from the twelve families in the block perished in the explosion. And while Annie Liggins later became Annie Welsh, her friends affectionately knew her as "Ashpan Annie" for the rest of her life. Unfortunately Benjamin Henneberry failed to locate any of his children.

While there were scenes of triumphant reunion and miraculous survival, tragic scenes were all too common. The Moore family had three children: Hazel, age nine; Gerald, age five; and Hilda, age six months. Their father was working at the North Street Railway Station and was unhurt in the explosion, but his wife and three children were in their house on

Two year-old Annie Liggins in hospital after being rescued the day after the blast. Sergeant Major Davies was in charge of the rescue effort and wrote on the back of the photo, "Annie Liggins (Ashpan baby). Rescued after being buried for 26 hr under debris of house. Compliments of Co. Sergeant Major Davies. Machine Gunner. 63rd HR."

Barrington Street when the blast went off. Mrs. Moore was taken to the hospital and later released, but to her horror, her three children had disappeared and were never heard from again. She was able to find the names Gerald and Hazel Moore on a ship's manifest but despite travelling to other ports including Boston, Mrs. Moore was never able to ever locate any of her children.

SANTA CLAUS LIMITED

Amid the grief, Christmas was approaching. In the December 17 issue of the *Daily Echo*, a front-page appeal for funds ran to give the sick kids in hospitals "the best Christmas they ever had." The newspaper noted that up to ten thousand children had been adversely affected by the explosion, and also appealed to children outside Halifax to give up their own presents to help the less fortunate. "The Sunshine Club" was the newspaper's children's section and began promoting the appeal. Soon other newspapers picked up the call and were also encouraging citizens to support local merchants and improve the economy by purchasing gifts for injured and homeless kids.

A few days later, the Halifax Board of Trade established Santa Claus Limited, a kind of telethon fundraising project with the goal of raising $5,000, enough money to purchase ten thousand Christmas packages—one for each of the children. Two telephones were installed at the project's headquarters in the Halifax Academy—the only school not seriously damaged in the explosion—and people could, perhaps for the first time in Halifax, call in pledges. Two hundred women volunteered and many other citizens with automobiles agreed to deliver the packages containing an assortment of fruit, cake, and candy.

Christmas trees were put up in the hospitals and the temporary convalescing sites. In addition to "The Sunshine Club" and Santa Claus Limited, many other groups and organizations pitched in

Christmas Cheer postcard, December 1917. The card is postmarked December 11, 1917, and is addressed to Miss Ruth Eisenhower, Springfield, Massachusetts.

and put on full Christmas meals with all the trimmings in an attempt to bring some measure of joy to the young survivors. The Overseas Club on board the *Lord Kelvin* in the harbour put on a special children's dinner featuring turkey, ice cream, and a surprise gift box for every child.

It was no doubt the worst of times for some young children; yet the kind acts of charity made some forget their sadness for a time and appreciate the real meaning of Christmas.

HERALD

HONEST ADVERTISING.

Nova S
Win-th
Newsp

MBER 10, 1917

VOLUME XLIII.

MOMEN

Practically All the Germans in Halifax Are To Be Arrest

ONE MILLION DOLLARS FROM DOMINION GOVERNMENT

Sir Robert Borden, who was in Halifax yesterday and leaves this morning to spend Monday in Kings County, announced that, pending full consideration of the needs of those who have suffered by the appalling calamity which has befallen Halifax, and, to a lesser degree, the neighboring town of Dartmouth, the Canadian Government has appropriated one million dollars for immediate relief. The amount thus provided will be immediately at the disposal of the Citizens' Finance Committee, or such other constituted authority as may be entrusted with the duty of administering the relief fund.

Sir Robert expects to arrive in Montreal on Wednesday and to be in Ottawa on Thursday.

THE MANAGING EXECUTIVE WITH FULL POWER

The citizens meeting on Saturday night appointed a permanent committee of twenty-two and these named an executive to be the cabinet and directing force. This executive consists of R. T. MacIreith, G. S. Campbell, Hon. R. G. Beazley, D. MacGillivary, A. E. Jones, H. R

Sixteen of
Taken Into C
Night and

The Deash Roll
to Grow and Now
Believed the Nun
Will Pass, 2,00

Sir Robert Borde
nounces $1,000,000
Dominion Govern
For Immediate R

HALIFAX, Decem

d the old
and the
use and
peared in
t yet fully
ge to ship-
f a very
ors every-
in many
ses were
which at
ce of the
class and
and fire
the explos-
en hundred
thus been

CHAPTER 15

WHO'S TO BLAME?

THE PRESS WAS QUICK TO demand answers as to how such a disaster could have happened. "Who is guilty?" asked the *Halifax Herald*, stating in no uncertain terms: "Let justice be done tho' the heavens fall." The day after the explosion the *Truro Daily News* demanded the "party or parties responsible [...] should be hung in good old fashion style at the yard's arm."

The first culprit identified by a hysterical city blown to pieces and fighting a world war was aliens. Since the outbreak of the war, Germans living in the city had been required to report to authorities once a month but now rumours were circulating that Germans had conspired to blow up the harbour. Newspapers fuelled the public's appetite for revenge, including one headline by the *Halifax Herald* on December 10 claiming, Practically All the Germans in Halifax Are To Be Arrested. In fact, a number of German citizens were threatened and punched in the streets, and a house on Young Street was torn apart by an angry mob. Sixteen Germans already registered with military authorities were jailed. But when it became clear that two ships in the harbour had collided resulting in the massive explosion, only so much vitriol could be directed towards people of German extraction. This, of course, led to the next question: were either of the ships to blame?

GERMAN SABOTAGE?

Hatred of all things German had already been intense before the explosion. Wounded and permanently scarred veterans had been returning from the front by the thousands, and in the spring of 1917, the United States entered the war. German U-boats began attacking convoys in North American waters in an all-out effort to destroy the Allies' supply lines. The two anti-submarine nets that had been deployed in Halifax Harbour were common in ports around Europe and North America, and rumours of German spies circulated everywhere. Some incidents of sabotage had occurred around New York, and a German national had exploded dynamite on the Vanceboro Bridge connecting Maine with New Brunswick. And so it was the opinion of many that Germans caused the Halifax Explosion.

Much of the so-called German treachery was simply silly rumours such as the story in Dartmouth that Henry Rosenberg, the retired principal of the Victoria School of Art and Design (now NSCAD), spied on ships in the harbour with a telescope from a tower atop his Crichton Avenue home. That Rosenberg, with his foreign-sounding name, would be up to treason at his picturesque home was unfounded, yet such was the mistrust and paranoia around the port in wartime.

With the *Halifax Herald* claiming the day after the explosion "Behind all, as responsible for the disaster, is that arch criminal, the Kaiser of Germany," it seemed reasonable to round up all the German people and put them in jail. And while nothing could be proved about German involvement with the explosion, one detail remained puzzling: why had the *Imo* behaved so erratically on the morning of December 6? William Hayes was one of the most experienced pilots in Halifax Harbour and had such a stellar reputation that Pilot Francis Mackey believed the Belgian vessel was not following Hayes's orders. Had Hayes—and maybe even Captain From—been murdered while one of the treacherous crewmembers took control of the vessel, steering it into the *Mont Blanc*?

The lone surviving crewmember aboard the helm of the *Imo* was John Johansen. He had been arrested while recovering at Bellevue Hospital for "acting suspiciously." Further investigation revealed Johansen had merely been anxious to get his hands on a newspaper to read about the accusations that he was a German infiltrator. Although he did also attempt to give a nurse money in exchange for his freedom. In the subsequent investigation, Johansen insisted that both Captain From and Pilot Hayes had remained on the bridge throughout the whole ordeal.

No collaborating evidence supported Johansen's testimony, since others on the bridge had perished and, in the end, no clear understanding of the *Imo*'s bizarre actions was reached. Yet public sentiment demanded retribution; because Johansen was considered a German—he was Norwegian—he was kept under armed guard while he testified at the wreck commission.

In the end, both the Canadian Supreme Court and the British Privy Council ruled the collision an accident and found no evidence of German foul play.

1917 WRECK COMMISSION

A week after the disaster, an inquiry known as the 1917 Wreck Commission opened in the Spring Garden Road courthouse, which was still damaged from the blast. Without electricity and with the windows boarded up, the oil lamps gave the courthouse a certain Victorian flare. Justice Arthur Drysdale, a Supreme Court judge and Nova Scotia's judge in admiralty, chaired the wreck commission, and all other parties had their own legal representation. Although the proceedings were not a criminal trial, they were nonetheless attempting to affix blame.

The legal talent on all sides was significant: Two expert mariners, Captain Louis A. Demers and Captain Walter Hose of the

Canadian Navy, assisted Judge Drysdale; William Henry represented the Canadian government; Charles Burchell represented the owners of *Imo*; Humphrey Mellish and J. P. Nolan the *Mont Blanc*; F. H. Bell for the city of Halifax; T. R. Robertson for the Halifax Pilotage Commission; and Andrew Cluney, Crown Prosecutor, for the Province of Nova Scotia.

Cold and damp, the old courthouse was partly empty when Justice Drysdale called the session to order. But public expectations ran high as the *Herald*'s headline cried out: Some One Blundered—Who? Court May Decide.

CAPTAIN LE MÉDEC'S TESTIMONY

Captain Aimé Le Médec of the *Mont Blanc* was the first witness called. Under examination from William Henry for the Canadian government, Le Médec, speaking through an interpreter, assured the court that no liquor had been allowed on board his vessel since the outbreak of the war. He explained in detail the loading of munitions in New York and his instructions to sail to Halifax to find a convoy to join for the crossing to France. Captain Le Médec then stated that the *Mont Blanc* had sailed through the harbour in its "rightful waters," about 150 metres from the Dartmouth shore, until sighting the *Imo* on the starboard side coming into their channel at about 8:25 A.M.

Captain Le Médec then stated that Pilot Mackey ordered—and he confirmed—one whistle, a cut in speed, and a move slightly to starboard. But *Imo* responded with two whistles, indicating it was moving toward the Dartmouth shore as well. The captain claimed this situation was repeated with the same outcome; *Imo* demanded his channel. But *Mont Blanc*, now having stopped its engines, could move no further to starboard lest it grind into the shore. Le Médec estimated he was no more than 50 or 60 metres from the shoreline and about 150 metres from the *Imo*.

With the *Imo* heading straight toward them, Le Médec gave orders for the only option left to him: swing the other way, to port, and toward Halifax. *Mont Blanc* issued two short blasts to indicate its intention, but suddenly *Imo* gave three whistles, and also moved toward the Halifax side. Accordingly, a collision now seemed inevitable. Yet Henry drilled Le Médec on the notion that perhaps the whistles were being misunderstood: perhaps they were indicating the local pilot's wishes and not questioning the other ship's course. Le Médec replied that both pilots were veteran harbour mariners and knew well each other's signals.

Le Médec, knowing the more explosive TNT was in his second hold, ordered full engines astern to try and avoid being hit there. Consequently, the *Imo* plunged three or four metres into the first hold, where the supposedly "less flammable" picric acid was stored. As it turned out, the picric acid was more flammable than TNT in a direct collision. Smoke and fire appeared, and Le Médec claimed it was impossible to put out the flames.

Certain his ship would explode, Le Médec maintained his duty was to try and save the men aboard. He ordered them to abandon ship and they quickly took to the lifeboats. After they arrived on the Dartmouth shore about twenty minutes later, the explosion erupted in the harbour. Only one crewmember was seriously hurt and later died.

Lawyer for the *Imo* Charles Burchell then began his cross-examination by asking Captain Le Médec if he was flying the red flag that morning. The captain replied that no, he was not because, as per international wartime rules, the red flag was only flown when explosives were being handled not transported. After Le Médec admitted that the burning *Mont Blanc* was drifting toward the Halifax piers when they abandoned it, Burchell wanted to know why they did not stay and try to alter the freighter's course. The captain then claimed he did try and stay, but the first officer demanded he go into the lifeboat. Even if he had remained, Le Médec explained, it would have been useless since the smoke was too heavy to see where the vessel was headed. For courtroom effect, Burchell made a point of calling the *Mont Blanc* the "French ship" and referred to the captain as a "crazy Frenchman."

Charles Burchell became more aggressive in his questioning. Perhaps he knew that with the *Imo*'s captain and pilot dead, he was the only one able to clear the *Imo* of blame. He challenged Le Médec on the command structure with Pilot Mackey on board and asked if the language barrier had given rise to any misunderstandings. Le Médec calmly replied that no such confusion occurred, and with his many years of sailing experience he knew all commands in both French and English.

Next, the lawyer for the city, F. H. Bell, wanted to know what had been done to attempt to put out the fire—had they let in any water, for example? But Le Médec replied that such an attempt would have taken at least a half hour. Additionally, their pumps were so small that it would have been fruitless to sprinkle water on the flames. He also maintained it was not safe to pour water on benzol.

Charles Burchell had assisted in the relief work and was well aware of the prevailing view throughout Halifax and Dartmouth that those aboard the *Mont Blanc* had cut and run without warning the unsuspecting public of the high explosives aboard their ship. In fact, civic emotion ran high against the crew of the *Mont Blanc*, and Le Médec required police protection while he remained in Halifax. Burchell had already declared early in the inquiry that responsibility lay with the two pilots: "whether both or one are at fault—they are responsible for the whole accident." Since Pilot Hayes was dead, it was clear Pilot Mackey was on trial along with his French colleagues. And Burchell showed no mercy when Francis Mackey took the stand.

FRANCIS MACKEY'S TESTIMONY

Pilot Francis Mackey confirmed Le Médec's testimony, but Burchell pointed out that there had been plenty of time between the collision and the explosion to warn people of the danger and nothing was attempted. Mackey objected, saying the men in the lifeboats yelled warnings as they rowed away from their burning ship. Attempting to frame Mackey and the Frenchmen as cowards, Burchell noted that many sailors, including the captain of the *Stella Maris*, were killed attempting to extinguish the fire on board the *Mont Blanc* while Mackey and the crew sailed away. The very day of the hearing, December 17, ninety-five unidentified dead were being buried. "Do you know the bells are ringing now for the funeral?" asked Burchell. Mackey replied calmly, "I have not heard them," but the damage to his reputation had been done. Burchell also took issue with the fact that Mackey was still working in the harbour while this cloud of doubt about his reputation remained.

Burchell then tried to have Mackey admit to perjury—lying under oath—and failing that, attacked Mackey for alleged drunkenness for which no proof was offered. And while Pilot Mackey thought highly of his fellow pilot, the deceased Pilot Hayes, it came out under questioning by Crown prosecutor Andrew Cluney that Mackey had piloted for the *Imo*'s Captain From more than once and did not think highly of his competence as a ship's captain.

OTHER TESTIMONY

One *Imo* crewman from the bridge, John Johansen, had survived the explosion and his testimony confirmed that SS *Clara* had first passed between the *Imo* and the Halifax shore. Johansen confirmed it was the *Stella Maris* that forced the *Imo* toward the Dartmouth shore. But other than admitting to seeing *Mont Blanc* approaching in the distance and confirming that Pilot Hayes had yelled to

Captain From that a collision was imminent, Johansen was vague about the events aboard the *Imo*. The question of whistle signals back and forth was particularly frustrating, as Johansen claimed, "a man at the wheel does not pay attention to whistles."

The testimony of those in charge of the harbour traffic was shocking. Captain Frederick Pasco had been acting superintendent of the dockyard while Commander Captain Edward Martin was away. He explained—in glowing terms—the improvement in policies and practices since the explosion, but the inquiry was more interested in procedures prior to the disaster. Pasco admitted the port was hard pressed to find adequate pilots or get the ones they had to co-operate fully due to the wartime boom. As well, Pasco admitted that hazardous goods were handled in routine fashion and many rules were regularly ignored in favour of expediency. Pasco insisted he had not been notified that a munitions ship would be arriving in the harbour that morning, and thought the amount of explosives on board was dangerous: "like a piece of fireworks ready to be exploded."

Toward the end of his testimony, Captain Pasco surprised the inquiry by noting Frederick Wyatt had told him the *Imo* had not received his permission to leave the harbour. As Chief Examining Officer, Wyatt alone had the authority to halt the ship from exiting the harbour.

Wyatt's testimony was similarly alarming. He claimed he had given direct instructions to the pilotage commission that he was to be notified of all movements in and out of the harbour, and he had given no permission for any ships to leave the harbour on the morning of December 6. He also claimed that had he known the *Imo* was heading outbound, he would have attempted to stop it. He admitted it was quite common for pilots to disobey his direct orders, and that this was hard to counter since pilots were regulated by the pilotage authority. And while Wyatt knew a munitions ship was coming in, he did not know it was carrying benzol.

Examining Officer Terrence Freeman testified that he had

given the *Mont Blanc* permission to proceed into the Bedford Basin on the morning of December 6, but with the provision that if there were any other ships exiting the harbour, his commanding officer (CXO Wyatt) would instruct him to halt all incoming vessels. No such instructions were given. Freeman knew the *Mont Blanc* was a munitions freighter, but he was not familiar with the super fuel benzol.

Imo lawyer Charles Burchell sparred quite vigorously with CXO Frederick Wyatt over the latter's assertion that *Imo* left the basin for the sea without his permission. Burchell claimed Pilot Hayes, now deceased, was being unfairly attacked without the possibility to defend himself. Wyatt insisted the sailing was not warranted. Burchell retorted that he had personally spoken with four different pilots that had not been reporting to their CXO for months.

In fact, Burchell was later able to confirm that for almost six months, not a single report had been sent from the pilotage office to the CXO. In addition, the pilotage office was administered by a fifteen-year-old boy, Edward Beazley, who was not bothering to phone in the various ship movements. In effect, Burchell had established beyond a doubt that CXO Wyatt's office was incompetent. The next day, Halifax newspapers had a field day demanding justice and offering new theories about the causes of the explosion.

The sensationalized reporting resulted in some sensitive military information being published—warship names and their movements, which shocked wartime censors. Justice Drysdale then issued a reprimand, claiming newspaper reporting of wartime secrets needed to stop. Yet CXO Wyatt was concerned he would be made the scapegoat and maintained his claim that the naval authorities had no jurisdiction over the pilots. His superiors had told him—this pointed directly to Superintendent Martin—that Ottawa was not prepared to interfere with the pilotage situation in Halifax. He claimed to have put his concerns in writing to his commander and thus was not responsible for any accidents despite fearing "an accident or collision was coming."

It was astonishing testimony. As evidence, Wyatt produced letters he had written to warn his superiors of the situation. Captain Superintendent Martin, upon returning to Halifax, claimed to be unaware of any such letters. Before the inquiry wrapped up, Acting Superintendent Pasco suspended CXO Wyatt from duty for a different incident in the harbour where a cargo ship and an oil tanker almost collided.

Meanwhile members of the public, incited by the newspapers' demands for answers, were still nervous about harbour traffic—especially munitions ships. In one exchange on December 29 between Ottawa cabinet minister C. C. Ballantyne, responsible for marine and naval affairs, and Halifax mayor P. F. Martin, the latter asked the former point-blank who was in charge of the Halifax Harbour. Martin claimed to have been unable to get an answer after two weeks of asking the same question. Attempting to restore public confidence and defend his Canadian naval authorities, Ballantyne insisted his administration of the port had not been careless and in fact, Halifax was the "best regulated port in any part of Canada." When Ballantyne returned to Ottawa, few Haligonians were convinced of the politician's statement. Neither were they willing to accept that Admiral Kingsmill, the RCN's chief in Ottawa, had placed competent naval leadership in the port.

It didn't help that a few days after the explosion, smoke was seen billowing out of the *Picton*, a damaged steamer with munitions aboard that had beached in Eastern Passage. But under the direction of Rear Admiral Chambers, the Halifax Rifles 63rd Regiment boarded the vessel, put the fire out, unloaded the ammunition, and secured the steamer. The *Picton* was later repaired and sent to sea. It helped somewhat to calm a nervous public that a second explosion was avoided and the dangerous situation was deftly handled.

THE VERDICT

On February 4, after hearing from more than fifty witnesses, Justice Drysdale released his decisions from the Wreck Commissioner's Inquiry. Drysdale's report was sent to Ottawa where Prime Minister Robert Borden ordered the thirteen findings released to the public. And Drysdale's conclusions were surprising.

While Drysdale concluded that the collision was the result of the violation of the rules of navigation, his third conclusion stated: "the pilot and master of the steamship *Mont Blanc* were wholly responsible for violating the rules of the road." Justice Drysdale further noted that Pilot Mackey, for reasons of gross negligence, should be "dismissed by the pilotage authorities and his licence cancelled." He recommended Mackey be investigated for criminal prosecution. As well, Drysdale proposed that the French authorities cancel Captain Le Médec's licence and that he be dealt with according to French law for "gross negligence," plus the fact that both he and Pilot Mackey failed to warn the public of a "probable explosion." Drysdale also concluded that CXO Frederick Wyatt was guilty of neglect in performing his duties, and Pilot Edward Renner of the SS *Clara* deserved censor for violating the "rules of the road."

Yet many in the community still thought that port or starboard be dammed, the Royal Canadian Navy authorities that allowed *Mont Blanc* to proceed unescorted into the harbour while the *Imo* was allowed to exit, were running the port, and were therefore responsible.

While plenty of Haligonians agreed with Drysdale's conclusion that it was unfair that almost everyone aboard *Mont Blanc* escaped injury while many *Imo* crewmen died, it was unexpected that the *Imo* was not considered at least partly to blame for the collision. Perhaps the bitter conscription war raging across Canada—with most of the opposition coming from French Canada—tainted Justice Drysdale's decision. Certainly it impacted the sentiment on the streets of Halifax. The public seemed convinced that the

Frenchmen aboard the burning freighter had behaved cowardly in saving themselves and failing to warn people of the looming explosion.

One clue into Drysdale's thinking can be gleaned from Captain Louis Demers's correspondence with Prime Minister Robert Borden. Demers, a mariner expert who had advised Justice Drysdale on navigational matters, insisted those aboard the *Mont Blanc* knew they were carrying high explosives and should have immediately turned to port upon hearing *Imo* sound two whistles claiming the Dartmouth side. It was *Mont Blanc*'s only proper course of action, claimed Demers, and certainly Justice Drysdale agreed.

Yet how and why the two vessels ended up facing each other in the same channel was also a key piece of the puzzle, and pointed to administration problems within the CXO's office.

The daily newspapers cried for heads to roll. Both Mackey and Le Médec were arrested after leaving the court on February 4 and Frederick Wyatt was seized the next day. All were charged with manslaughter. Wyatt and Le Médec were released on bail, but Mackey couldn't raise the $6,000 (and had no hope of earing it, as he was suspended from his pilot duties as a government-appointed investigation examined the pilotage situation in Halifax).

INQUIRIES, APPEALS, AND COUNTER-CLAIMS

The government inquiry into the pilotage authority in Halifax found corruption among the pilots was widespread; overcharging, kickback commissions, and minimal reporting were common. The inquiry recommended an extensive reorganization.

Within days of the inquiry closure, and before Justice Drysdale released his findings, the Royal Canadian Navy restructured its operation in Halifax. It installed a new chief superintendent transferred from Esquimalt, British Columbia, Vice Admiral C. W. Story, and Captain Edward Martin was sent west to replace Story. CXO Frederick Wyatt was permanently removed from his post and Captain Pasco was transferred to Saint John, New Brunswick.

Shipments of munitions and high explosives continued to pass through Halifax Harbour for the remainder of the war, but new regulations and procedures made everything much safer and all pilots began co-operating fully with the navy's leadership.

Yet all was not done in the matter of who was to blame. As the owners of the two vessels filed claims and counterclaims, the case progressed to the Admiralty Court, where Justice Drysdale again headed the proceedings. He handled down the same verdict: *Mont Blanc* was solely at fault.

The owners of the *Mont Blanc* then launched an appeal to the Supreme Court of Canada that ended on May 19, 1919, with two judges siding with Justice Drysdale, two placing the blame solely on the *Imo,* and a fifth judge, Justice Anglin, ruling that both vessels were equally responsible. A final appeal to the Privy Council in England—then the ultimate judicial authority—ended with the council agreeing that each vessel was equally at fault. The Privy Council determined that once the vessels were within five hundred feet of each other, universal maritime law dictated that both vessels reverse engines, and this did not happen. Thus both were equally blameworthy.

Captain Le Médec, Pilot Mackey, and Chief Examining Officer Wyatt had all been charged with manslaughter, but Mackey and Le Médec were eventually exonerated after a preliminary trial and a writ of habeas corpus—a complaint of unlawful detention—was filed and approved. Frederick Wyatt would also have his day in court.

Francis Mackey was villainized by the Halifax press and fought for some time to be reinstated as a pilot. In fact, Benjamin Russell, the judge who heard the preliminary trial later, made it clear what he thought about Mackey's conduct on December 6: "the defendant had taken every possible care to prevent the collision which was about to be caused by the conduct of the *Imo*." Russell's verdict, however, was attacked on the streets of Halifax.

Due to public anger, both the federal government in Ottawa and local naval officials in Halifax delayed restoring Mackey's licence for four years; in 1922 he was allowed to resume his piloting duties in the Halifax Harbour. Although he was legally exonerated, Francis Mackey was "made the goat" partly due to local pressure and the reluctance for government officials in Ottawa to shoulder any of the blame. Yet Mackey never quite outlived his association with the Halifax Explosion. He retired in 1937 with a yearly pension of $1,600 and died in 1961. His obituary made mention of his piloting the vessel that "exploded, taking the lives of 2,000 people."

Frederick Wyatt appeared before a grand jury on April 16, 1918, and was acquitted after Justice Russell instructed the jury that "there was nothing in the eyes of the law to justify the charge of manslaughter." Wyatt, however, was still vilified by the public and was given a personal discharge from the Royal Canadian Navy. He moved far away from Halifax. Although he was the lone Royal Canadian Navy figure to suffer personally from the Halifax Explosion, the reputation of the entire institution was damaged.

Captain Aimé Le Médec, for his part, resumed his nautical career without any serious interruption until he passed away in the 1930s. The *Imo* was refloated in 1918, repaired, and became a whaler with a new name: *Guvernoren*. The vessel struck a rock near the Falkland Islands in 1921, and while the crew survived, the old vessel did not. It went down in the South Atlantic.

CHAPTER 16

REORGANIZING AND RECONSTRUCTING

In December 1917, the Dominion Exhibition Building held a Christmas gift show but on the morning of the explosion, it sat empty. The building was extensively damaged and during the summer of 1919, a custodian's body was discovered in the rubble, the last body recovered from the explosion. The ground became home to temporary housing and today is part of the Halifax Forum complex.

SIX WEEKS AFTER THE EXPLOSION, the Dominion government, under the War Measures Act, formed the Halifax Relief Commission (HRC). Provincial and city officials had recommended a federal agency be instituted to manage and administrate the remaining relief funds as well as the major reconstruction efforts going forward. Nova Scotia Premier George Murray readily agreed that the ad hoc relief committees had done admirable work but now a more organized approach with more resources was necessary. Members of the commission included: businessman Ralph Bell, secretary; lawyer Sherman Rogers, chairman; William Wallace, county judge; and Frederick Fowke, an Ontario merchant. The HRC's power was substantial: "take over and receive all unexpended moneys and goods contributed for the relief of the residents of Halifax, Dartmouth, and vicinity who suffered by reason of the disaster of December 6 last."

Later, the province gave the commission additional powers to "repair, rebuild, or restore any building or property damaged, destroyed, or lost in or by reason of said disaster, or compensate the owner thereof, or any person having an interest therein in respect thereof to such an extent as the commission may think fit." Such unlimited powers were controversial; the commission's decisions trumped both private and municipal stakeholders in all financial or property matters.

A lot had been already accomplished. Almost five thousand people had registered their losses—this number would eventually triple—the medical team had dealt with thousands of victims, and the inventories of supplies including clothing were in good supply. The finance committee—supported by a line of credit from the Bank of Nova Scotia—had substantial resources and a strong bookkeeping system. The mortuary at the school on Chebucto Road had been mostly cleared out, and the transportation committee had succeeded in moving victims to secure sites while even managing to erect a large vehicle garage.

Yet the ongoing task of getting a devastated community of fifty thousand back on their feet was enormous. The commission's mandate was laid out: provide temporary assistance, support the injured, and undertake compensation for property and human loss, while also taking on the reconstruction of shattered areas. As the need for emergency services declined, the commission's main focus became rehabilitation, finance, medical, and rebuilding. Cash allowances—to offset everything from funeral services, medical bills, and living expenses—began to be paid out based on a number of factors. Some of these factors included previous wages for victims now unable to work, destitute families left without a wage earner, and even long-term disabilities gained as a result of the explosion.

One of Halifax's most well-known institutions prior to the explosion was the city's School for the Blind, under the direction of Frederick Fraser. After the explosion, over one thousand cases of serious eye damage were reported and Fraser's institution was quickly overwhelmed with applicants. Fraser launched an appeal for half a million dollars in donations. He was then able to hire extra staff and open an eye client for victims, all while teaching his new students how to live with their disability. But the need was so great that in the spring, the commission hired a New York couple, Mr. and Mrs. Joseph Murphy, to come to Halifax and take charge of the blind relief effort.

The Murphys established classes teaching self-reliance and skill development with the goal that blind and partially sighted individuals could lead productive lives. Compensation—paid out from the substantial HRC fund—for blind men was $50 a month, but women received only $30 per month. Adults who lost one eye got $30 per year. Children who had fully lost their sight or had been partially impaired got their schooling paid for and a $100 flat-fee payment when they turned twenty-one.

Overall the full HRC donation fund amounted to an astonishing $27 million. Even though the total losses reported were $35 million, insurance and other payments helped lessen the blow. Still, there persisted a notion that the commission was flush with money and was not keen on paying pensions to ordinary sufferers. Protesters of the HRC claimed the commission was quite willing to pay fees to medical groups and social workers, but not so much to victims.

That being said, the commission's motto was "relief, not compensation" and was generally frugal with its payouts. For instance: a widow with a husband who had earned $110 a month would receive a monthly pension of $40, plus an additional $8 for each dependant. And if said widow owned property valued above $3,000, she could expect a clawback on that $40. Yet factories, churches, and homeowners all received some sort of compensation; the Acadia Sugar Refinery, for instance, received $190,000—significant, but not enough to fund a full rebuild. Monetary reimbursement for property losses was considered revolutionary since at the time, American relief efforts did not include this sort of compensation.

DARTMOUTH RELIEF COMMITTEE

Dartmouth's destruction was less severe than Halifax's—perhaps one hundred deaths were recorded. Yet the town managed to establish a separate relief committee under the direction of former Mayor A. C. Johnston. The Dartmouth Relief Committee (DRC) formed quickly at the ferry terminal on December 6, and was headquartered initially in the nearby post office. It then moved to Greenvale School, and finally to Christ Church parish hall. Various subcommittees to address all pressing issues—medical care, food, shelter, mortuary, security, transportation, and fuel—were established, but without hospital facilities the major issue was medical services.

The Nova Scotia Hospital—which treated mental illnesses—did manage to acquire military doctors as well as out-of-town physicians, and treated over two hundred patients the first day. Edgemere House on Crichton Avenue, Greenvale School, and Dr. Daniel Parker's Beechwood estate (later an infectious disease facility) all became temporary hospitals. A number of doctors treated victims in their own homes. The DRC opened food depots in the hard-hit north end and even beyond the town's boundaries at

The damaged cordage plant after the explosion.

Tufts Cove. Food disbursement was restricted to one week's supply, but deserving victims could reapply weekly. Since the Halifax relief group had received the bulk of national and international donations, funds and supplies were sent from Halifax across the harbour.

By the end of January 1918, the state of emergency had stabilized and the relief committee moved from Greenvale School to the Christ Church Parish Hall, allowing children to return to school. Greenvale and Hawthorne schools, both constructed with brick, had withstood the blast. With intricate scheduling, the two schools continued to educate all the children of Dartmouth. And in the fall of 1918, with much of the relief effort complete and most of the ongoing financial support (survivor pensions, etc.) administered by HRC, the Halifax Relief Commission took over the Dartmouth committee.

Canadian Hydro-Stone Plant, Eastern Passage, c.1919. Sand for the blocks came from a large sandy beach called Barrie Beach, also known as Land's End, near Shore Road. Manufactured at Eastern Passage, the hydrostone blocks were transported by narrow-gauge railway and then on floating barges to north end Halifax.

CHAPTER 17

THE REBUILD

WHEN THE HALIFAX RELIEF COMMISSION was established on January 22, 1918, three thousand homes had been repaired, but by the end of January, almost five thousand people were still homeless. The HRC decided to bring in large numbers of workmen to clear much of devastated Richmond and rebuild the area. Colonel Robert Low was hired as chairman of the reconstruction committee. His two responsibilities included repairing existing homes and building temporary housing for the homeless, which was desperately needed. Under Colonel Low's direction, the reconstruction group cleared out many of the damaged buildings on the Exhibition Grounds off Almon Street. Forty two-storey apartment buildings were erected on the grounds, constructed out of wood and tarpaper with beaverboard inside.

In total, 320 units were constructed and 2,200 tenants were inside by March. Named in honour of the Governor of Massachusetts, Samuel W. McCall, the Governor McCall apartments were built to last five years and featured electricity and sewers. Furniture was provided free of charge as part of the relief donations from Massachusetts. Temporary apartments were also erected on the Garrison Grounds near Citadel Hill, the South Commons on Bell Road, and in Victoria Park in Dartmouth.

Rents were between $5 and $12 per month. The relief commission built a community centre in the McCall village with assistance from other agencies, including the YMCA, the Imperial Order Daughters of the Empire (IODE), and the Christian Science relief fund. The transient village was quite successful, with one notable exception: many people were living in close quarters, and the smallpox outbreak in the summer of 1918 hit the community quite hard. Yet as a major seaport, Halifax was familiar with smallpox outbreaks and was able to placard the affected homes and isolated the infectious disease. By fall, the epidemic had subsided.

THE HYDROSTONE

"A new and thoroughly modern city underway in the north of Halifax…Men say the day of miracles is passed but there is a vision of regeneration here that fringes the miraculous…The new city remains—and grows, building by building, street by street, amid the tumultuous music of a thousand hammers, the wholesome discord of a thousand caws." (Poster promoting the Hydrostone development in 1919.)

Named in honour of Massachusetts benefactor Governor Samuel McCall, the temporary apartments provided homes for three thousand victims.

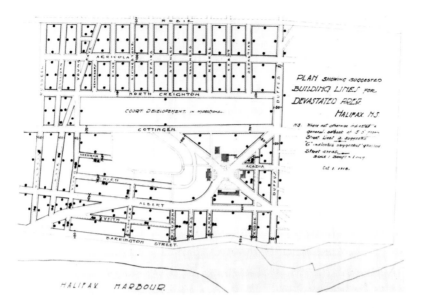

Plan for the north-end rebuild, October 1, 1918. The Hydrostone became popular and eventually all 324 units were rented out to tenants. The *Evening Echo* published a number of praises written by students from the nearby Alexander Mackay and Richmond schools including this one: "I like my new home. I am not afraid of fire in the night there."

Merkelsfield was a north-end area of about 130 hectares bordered by Young, Gottingen, Duffus, and Agricola streets. Prior to the explosion, the Halifax Land Company had partially developed the district with housing but the blast ruined most of the homes. In order to rebuild permanent housing, the Halifax Relief Commission expropriated some of the land and hired English town planner Thomas Adams to develop a community. Along with architect George Ross—of the Ross and MacDonald architectural firm in Montreal—Adams devised what has been called the first "planned municipal community" in Canada.

Adams's vision was to make urban areas more liveable by including parks and public spaces alongside high-quality (yet affordable) housing. Adams also realigned the roads, but many old Richmond residents—who argued that money contributed to rebuilding their community was being wasted on a fanciful housing scheme—deemed his "garden city" concept too extravagant. Provincial and federal officials, however, were on the side of Adams and Ross. And so construction got underway in September 1918.

The main building material used was a new type of concrete that had been developed in Chicago. "Hydrostone" was a solid block containing gravel, church rock, sand, and Portland cement moulded under pressure and steam. The material was partly chosen because it was fire-resistant (should there be another disaster) but also because, at thirty-six kilograms, the blocks were workable without requiring heavy-lifting equipment.

The blocks were constructed at the Canadian Hydro-Stone Plant in Eastern Passage, where up to four thousand blocks could be produced on a good day. They were transported on a narrow-gauge railway to the Dartmouth waterfront, shipped across the harbour to Richmond, and then transported on another temporary railway up the hill to the building sites. Sand for the blocks came from Barrie Beach in Eastern Passage and so much was taken for construction that today, the beach consists entirely of rocks.

To create variety, six different layouts of four-unit townhouses were designed with a two-unit home at the end of each street. Roofs and exterior finishes were also varied to give each home a sense of uniqueness. Most of the ten blocks had homes that faced out across spacious boulevards with grass and trees offering play spaces for children. Electric and telephones poles were placed along rear alleyways that also offered parking.

Some units were ready as soon as 1919, and when completed in 1921, the Hydrostone neighbourhood consisted of 328 dwellings and about 2,000 tenants. Rents varied from $25 a month to $50 for the larger seven-room homes. Fifteen stores and three offices were also erected in a commercial site on Young Street, with the relief commission office at the corner of Young and Isleville Streets. Tenants of the commercial district included a pharmacy, a hardware store, a grocery, a boot and shoe shop, a tobacconist, a stationer, and the Royal Bank.

While a number of names were proposed for the family-focused community, "Hydrostone" became the only real name used for the development. While the commission managed and rented the Hydrostone for over two decades, it began selling off units to tenants in 1949. By the mid-1950s, all units were private property.

Despite the initial scepticism over Thomas Adams's grand design, Richmond residents generally thought highly of the finished Hydrostone community. One young boy, Robert Noble, who lost his father and brother in the explosion, wrote in the *Evening Echo* on February 10, 1921, "How I like the Hydrostone. I like my new home. I am not afraid of fire in the night there. The streets are cement and you don't have to tramp through mud. We can do our own shopping and save our carfare. The new Richmond School is nearly ready and is the finest in Eastern Canada." One small drawback, though, was that gardening was difficult since pieces of metal, no doubt fragments from the explosion, turned up nearly everywhere. Ross and MacDonald built a number of similar (free-standing) homes at both east and west ends of the Hydrostone. Devonshire and Dartmouth Avenues were laid running east toward the harbour, intersecting at what became Richmond Square, while the remaining areas of Merkelsfield above the Hydrostone were gradually in-filled.

But very little of the relief funds were used to help rebuild the damaged homes in Africville. After the Second World War, the relief commission worked with the city to develop Fort Needham overlooking Richmond, Africville, and the Bedford Basin into a public park. Yet little attention was paid to the African Nova Scotian community and years later, one Africville resident would recall that "when the payment ends, that's where Africville begins."

Richmond School looking north towards Bedford Basin from Fort Needham. Rockhead Prison is visible in the left top corner. The school was built on Devonshire and Dartmouth Avenues to replace the destroyed Richmond School on Roome Street.

The Halifax Relief Commission constructed about six hundred additional homes including in parts of north-end Dartmouth around Windmill Road and Hester and Fairbanks Streets. Still shaken from the explosion, a number of residents refused to return to live so close to the harbour. Overall Halifax's north end was not fully repopulated until the Second World War brought major population growth to the city.

Homes were not the only buildings in need of reconstruction after the explosion: churches and schools were also rebuilt, including the Richmond School. Renowned architect Andrew Cobb designed the new building, which still stands today as a provincial family court. It bears a bronze plaque dedicated to the memory of the eighty-eight students of Richmond School who died in the explosion. When the plaque was dedicated in 1924, however, many viewed it as controversial; some of the children had never been found and many of their families had not yet given up hope. Even the principal's own daughter had perished in the blast, yet Principal George Huggins had insisted, purchasing the plaque himself.

HALIFAX RELIEF COMMISSION

Entrusted with millions in relief funds, the relief commission remained financially strong even after the temporary and permanent homes had been erected and payouts to businesses and institutions had occurred. Pensions for victims and housing management became central concerns, but equally pressing was the preservation of funds so allowances could continue until all pensioners passed away. Retired army officer William Tibbs became secretary-comptroller as well as the most senior member after commissioners Rodgers and Wallace passed away in 1928. Tibbs remained with the HRC for a total of fifty-four years.

Much to the chagrin of the City of Halifax, the commission paid no property taxes on its Hydrostone properties but did contribute financially to a number of public projects in the north end, including turning Fort Needham into a memorial park in 1957. As well, in 1964, the HRC donated $100,000 to build the North End Memorial Library, featuring a sculpture designed to commemorate the victims of the explosion.

The Halifax Relief Commission office in the Hydrostone shopping district on the corner of Isleville Street (then North Creighton) and Young Street.

THE 1930S AND 40S

The Great Depression was tough on the Hydrostone—almost half the properties and most of the commercial operations were empty by the mid-1930s. Along with many other retailers, the Glube Brothers' store had been forced to close, but later, Joe Glube managed to open a successful furniture store on Gottingen Street that blossomed into a local furnishing store chain called Glubes.

The arrival of the Second World War brought an influx of residents and a shortage of rental units. Toward the end of the 1940s, properties were sold off to tenants creating a capital gain for the HRC and new property taxes for the city. One explosion victim, "Ashpan" Annie Liggins, then Annie Welsh, purchased a home with her family on Kane Street and remained in the Hydrostone for the rest of her life. And another child of the explosion, Jean Hunter, moved to the Hydrostone in the 1980s.

By the 1970s, it was clear the work of the Halifax Relief Commission was coming to an end. In 1976, with 61 pensioners still drawing funds—1,028 pensioners had begun receiving funds in 1920—the commission was officially dissolved after six decades of service. The federal Department of Veterans Affairs administrated the remaining funds with the provision that upon the death of all pensioners, all remaining money be transferred to the province or city for distribution within the damaged area. But by 2002, with 3 pensioners remaining, the money was completely spent, but the federal government continued to pay the three outstanding survivors. In 2010, the last pensioner passed away.

Today on the south end of Fort Needham, there stands a small cairn dedicated to the Halifax Relief Commission and the work its volunteers undertook to help the victims of the devastation.

CHAPTER 18

AN OLD CURSE

GROWING UP WITHIN SIGHT OF Halifax Harbour, many children were told an old Indigenous legend called the "Curse of the Narrows." It maintained that one evening long ago, a Mi'kmaw brave was watching from the shadows as his girlfriend secretly met a British officer. The couple escaped by canoe into the harbour at the Narrows, and the brave followed them by walking through a series of canoes lashed together. He caught up to the couple and, although the moon was hidden in the clouds, he killed the officer.

But when the moonlight returned, it was revealed that he had mistakenly slain his girlfriend and the British officer had escaped. Dismayed, the brave destroyed the canoes and placed a curse on the Narrows, claiming that the British would build three bridges across the Narrows and all would be destroyed: "Three a bridge over these waves shall rise, built by the pale face, so strong and wise, three times shall fall like a dying breath, in storm, in silence, and last in death."

Two bridges were in fact erected at the Narrows south of today's A. Murray MacKay Bridge. The first was a railway bridge that was completed in 1884 but collapsed in a hurricane in 1891. Two years later, a second bridge at the same location floated away on a strong tide. In 1970, the MacKay Bridge was completed across the Narrows and has stood ever since, despite warnings from many superstitious folks. Some people well versed in folklore claim that the curse was not specific to bridges, but only to the Narrows. In fact, they claim, the prediction of three disasters at the Narrows has now been completed: two bridges gave out and one explosion took place.

Aerial view of north-end Halifax after the rebuild, showing the Hydrostone district with Gottingen Street and Needham Hill on the right, c.1921.

CHAPTER 19

MONUMENTS AND COMMEMORATIONS

ALL FOUR RICHMOND CHURCHES—ST. JOSEPH'S Roman Catholic, St. Mark's Anglican, Grove Presbyterian, and Kaye Street Methodist—were destroyed in the Halifax Explosion. But three months later, what remained of the Grove Presbyterian and Kaye Street congregations began worshipping in a hastily constructed tarpaper building on Young Street (today, the space is a small park located directly across from the Hydrostone Market). A few years later, the Grove-Kaye Church came together to form the United Memorial Church. They constructed a new building—partly built on the foundation of the old Kaye Street Methodist Church—erected in 1921.

The church dedication included the presentation of bronze bells by survivor Barbara Orr, who played the carillon in the church tower. The bells were etched with a memorial to Barbara's family members who were lost in the tragedy. For five decades, the memorial bells were played on special occasions in the north end. Eventually, though, the heavy bells were considered structurally unsafe to remain in the tower. A new tower was needed and fundraising efforts began in 1983 to erect a new permanent memorial at Fort Needham.

MEMORIAL BELL TOWER

Two years later, the Memorial Bell Tower Monument—with the same bronze bells—was dedicated in Fort Needham Memorial

Memorial Park was dedicated in 1985 and features the same bronze bells from the 1921 United Memorial Church dedication plus an additional four bells donated in 1990.

Park, overlooking the waterfront site of the explosion. The monument, designed by Keith Graham, features an uneven crown suggesting the ragged ruins of the explosion. Once again, Barbara played the carillon. And since 1985, every year at 9:05 A.M. on December 6, the bells ring out in a memorial ceremony marking the tragedy.

On December 6 of that same year, survivor Millicent (Upham) Swindells and her granddaughter Anne Louis Ihasz placed a capsule of explosion-related items in the bell tower. Partially blinded in the blast, Millicent had lost her Rector Street home, her mother, two sisters, and a brother in 1917. There are hopes that on December 6, 2017, Anne will represent the Upham family at a similar ceremony when the time capsule will be opened to commemorate the one-hundredth anniversary of the explosion.

SCHOOLS IN RICHMOND

St. Joseph's Catholic Church on Gottingen Street—along with its convent and glebe house—was badly damaged in the explosion, but the church basement survived and was eventually used for services and classes. The Catholic girls' school on Kaye Street had almost 450 students enrolled at the time of the explosion (girls and boys), and was flattened in the blast. A total of 23 girls died that day—eight at the school itself, and another 15 at home. Boys were attending the same school in the afternoon at the time—their school had burned down prior to the disaster—and were mainly at home or outside during the explosion. Yet fifty-five Catholic boys lost their lives in the explosion. A new St. Joseph's School was later erected on Russell Street, which became the St. Joseph's-Alexander MacKay School after an educational merger in the 1970s.

The Halifax Protestant Orphanage on Veith Street—and its one-room classroom—was also destroyed in the explosion. Despite seeking refuge in the basement, twenty-five children and three adults died at the site. Today a "neighbourhood hub" called Veith House sits in the same spot, serving as a community centre and preschool.

The third school in the Richmond area, Bloomfield School on Agricola Street, was far enough away from the shore that its two buildings, while damaged, were not totally destroyed.

THE BOSTON CHRISTMAS TREE

Massachusetts had given so much—time, supplies, personnel, money—to Halifax's relief effort that in December of the following year, 1918, the city sent a giant Christmas tree to Boston as a thank you for its tremendous assistance. The tree was lavishly decorated and erected in the city centre on the Boston Commons.

In 1971, with hopes of promoting Nova Scotia-grown Christmas trees in New England, the Lunenburg County Christmas Tree Producers Association revived the tradition by donating a tree—in excess of sixteen metres tall and weighting two tons—to Boston. The Province of Nova Scotia eventually took over the project, and selecting and harvesting the perfect tree for Boston now takes place on the first Saturday in December every year. The process is broadcasted across the province, and the government chooses a family-owned business for the honour each year. The tree is then strapped onto a large truck and driven through Nova Scotia, New Brunswick, and Maine before reaching its final destination. Upon arrival, there is an official lightning ceremony—a symbolic goodwill gesture between the two communities—on the Boston Commons.

ONE HUNDRED YEARS LATER

Many events are planned to commemorate the centennial anniversary of the explosion on December 6, 2017. A commemorative stamp and coin are being produced, along with special concerts including a unique work by Symphony Nova Scotia. In addition, a documentary film on the Halifax School of the Deaf and its students during the explosion will be released, and at least two original plays, *The Lullaby Project* and *Extraordinary Acts*, are to be put on by local theatre companies. St. Paul's Anglican Church is planning a recreation of a memorial service for victims entitled *The Lost Memorial Project.*

But perhaps the most attention for the one hundredth anniversary of the tragedy has been directed towards revitalizing Fort Needham Memorial Park. The six-hectare public park—deeded to the city in 1942 on the condition it remain a public park forever—is situated high on a hill with magnificent views of the harbour including the Narrows, Dartmouth, and the Halifax Shipyard. The city is working to improve landscaping throughout, refurnish the monument and interpretive elements, and make the park more accessible. In addition, the bronze memorial bells will be repaired and tuned so a number of hymns and songs can be played remotely. Indeed, a full rededication of the park is planned for December 6, 2017, with the inclusion of a new time capsule, which will include a host of items including letters from dignitaries, the new coin and stamp, plus a number of artifacts from the actual explosion. And in 2016, the Halifax Explosion was declared a National Historic Event by Parks Canada since it is considered by many Canadians to be a "defining moment in Canadian history."

This 544-kilogram cannon from the stern of the *Mont-Blanc* was blasted three kilometres from the harbour to Little Albro Lake in Dartmouth. Today the cannon stands near the lake in Mont-Blanc Memorial Park at the corner of Albro Lake Road and Pinecrest Drive. A plaque lists the names of ninety-four people killed.

In front of the fire station at Lady Hammond Road near Robie Street, stands a memorial to the nine firefighters that died trying to reach the burning *Mont Blanc*. Inside the station hangs the steering wheel from the *Patricia* fire engine that Billy Wells drove that fateful day in 1917.

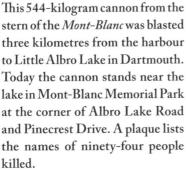

At Regatta Point on the Northwest Arm there remains a large fragment of the *Mont Blanc* anchor weighting 517 kilograms. It landed five kilometres from the ship and is today mounted on a cairn with the inscription: "The Dec.6 1917 Halifax Explosion hurled this 1140 lb anchor shaft 2.35 miles from the S.S. *Mont Blanc* to this park."

Historic monument to the Hydrostone district in the park on Young Street next to the Hydrostone Market. Erected by the Historic Sites and Monuments Board of Canada, the plaque states that the Hydrostone was "Canada's first government-assisted housing project."

BIBLIOGRAPHY

Armstrong, John. *The Halifax Explosion and the Royal Canadian Navy; Inquiry and Intrigue.* Vancouver: University of British Columbia Press, 2002.

Beed, Blair. *1917 Halifax Explosion and American Response.* Halifax: Nimbus Publishing, 2010.

Bird, Michael J. *The Town That Died.* Toronto: McGraw-Hill Ryerson, 1967.

Boileau, John. *Halifax and the Royal Canadian Navy.* Halifax: Nimbus Publishing, 2010.

Bruneau, Carol. *Glass Voices.* Toronto: Cormorant Books, 2007.

Canadian Manufacturers' Association. *The Industrial Ascendancy of Nova Scotia.* Halifax: Imperial Publicity Committee, 1913.

Chapman, Harry. *Dartmouth's Day of Sorrow: Halifax Harbour Explosion.* Dartmouth: Dartmouth Historical Association, 2007.

Griswold, A. W. *Thirty Views of the Dartmouth Disaster.* Dartmouth: A. W. Griswold, 1917.

Kitz, Janet and Joan Payzant. *December 1917: Re-visiting the Halifax Explosion.* Halifax: Nimbus Publishing, 2006.

Kitz, Janet. *Shattered City, The Halifax Explosion and the Road to Recovery.* Halifax: Nimbus Publishing, 1989.

Kitz, Janet. *Survivors: Children of the Halifax Explosion.* Halifax: Nimbus Publishing, 1992.

Laffoley, Steven. *The Blue Tattoo.* Lawrencetown Beach: Pottersfield Press, 2014.

MacDonald, Laura. *The Curse of the Narrows: the Halifax Explosion 1917.* New York: Walker and Company, 2005.

MacLennan, Hugh. *Barometer Rising.* Toronto: McClelland & Stewart, 1941.

MacNeil, Robert. *Burden of Desire.* New York: Doubleday, 1992.

Mahar, James and Rowena Mahar. *Too Many to Mourn, One Family's Tragedy in the Halifax Explosion.* Halifax: Nimbus Publishing, 1998.

Maybee, Janet. *Aftershock: the Halifax Explosion and the Persecution of Pilot Francis Mackey*. Halifax: Nimbus Publishing, 2015.

Metson, Graham and Archibald MacMechan. *The Halifax Explosion, December 6, 1917*. Toronto: McGraw-Hill Ryerson, 1978.

Parker, Mike, *The Smoke-Eaters, A History of Firefighting in Nova Scotia c.1750–1950*, Halifax, Nimbus Publishing, 2002.

Raddall, Thomas H. *In My Time*. Toronto: McClelland & Stewart, 1976.

Ruffman, Alan and Colin Howell. *Ground Zero: a Reassessment of the 1917 Explosion in Halifax Harbour*. Halifax: Nimbus Publishing, 1994.

Tattrie, Jon. *Black Snow*. Lawrencetown Beach: Pottersfield Press, 2009.

Weir, Gerald. *Devastated Halifax*. Halifax: Gerald Weir, 1917.

Whitehead, Ruth Holmes. *Tracking Doctor Lonecloud*. Fredericton: Goose Lane Editions, 2002.

Zemel, Joel. *Scapegoat: the Extraordinary Legal Proceedings Following the 1917 Halifax Explosion*. Halifax: SVP Productions, 2012.

IMAGE CREDITS

Nova Scotia Archives: 1, 3, 5, 8, 11, 13, 18, 27, 42, 44, 45, 46, 54, 55, 57, 63, 67, 69, 71, 73, 76, 82, 102, 104, 105, 108, 109, 112

Maritime Museum of the Atlantic: 79

National Archives of Canada: 68

Postcards: 10, 14, 16, 20, 23, 34, 37, 52, 64, 65, 70, 81, 97

The Industrial Ascendency of Nova Scotia (booklet): 49, 59

Devastated Halifax (booklet, 1917): 50, 53

30 Views of the Dartmouth Disaster (booklet, 1917): 74, 101

The Halifax Explosion, December 6, 1917 by Graham Metson: 31

INDEX

Numbers set in italics refer to images.

V

Victoria School of Art and Design
63, 84

W

War of 1812 9, 12
Windsor 60, 61
Wolfville 60, 61
Wreck Commission 85

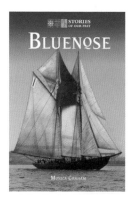

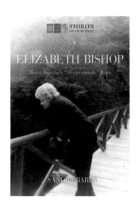
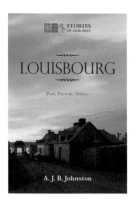
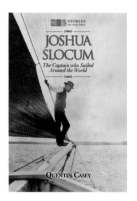
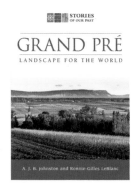
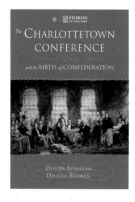

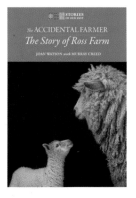